PREVENTING THE
EMOTIONAL ABUSE
AND NEGLECT OF
PEOPLE WITH
INTELLECTUAL DISABILITY

of related interest

Learning Difficulties and Sexual Vulnerability
A Social Approach
Andrea Hollomotz
ISBN 978 1 84905 167 5
eISBN 978 0 85700 381 2

Active Support
Enabling and Empowering People with Intellectual Disabilities
Jim Mansell and Julie Beadle-Brown
ISBN 978 1 84905 111 8
eISBN 978 0 85700 300 3

Safeguarding Adults and the Law
2nd edition
Michael Mandelstam
ISBN 978 1 84905 300 6
eISBN 978 0 85700 626 4

Understanding and Working with People with
Learning Disabilities Who Self-injure
Edited by Pauline Heslop and Andrew Lovell
ISBN 978 1 84905 208 5
eISBN 978 0 85700 443 7

How to Break Bad News to People with Intellectual Disabilities
A Guide for Carers and Professionals
Irene Tuffrey-Wijne
Foreword by Professor Baroness Sheila Hollins
ISBN 978 1 84905 280 1
eISBN 978 0 85700 583 0

Making Partnerships with Service Users and Advocacy Groups Work
How to Grow Genuine and Respectful Relationships in Health and Social Care
Julie Gosling and Jackie Martin
ISBN 978 1 84905 193 4
eISBN 978 0 85700 608 0

A Practical Guide to Delivering Personalisation
Person-Centred Practice in Health and Social Care
Helen Sanderson and Jaimee Lewis
ISBN 978 1 84905 194 1
eISBN 978 0 85700 422 2

Social Care, Service Users and User Involvement
Edited by Peter Beresford and Sarah Carr
Foreword by Simon Denegri
ISBN 978 1 84905 075 3
eISBN 978 0 85700 264 8

PREVENTING THE EMOTIONAL ABUSE AND NEGLECT OF PEOPLE WITH INTELLECTUAL DISABILITY

Stopping Insult and Injury

SALLY ROBINSON

Foreword by Hilary Brown

Jessica Kingsley *Publishers*
London and Philadelphia

First published in 2013
by Jessica Kingsley Publishers
116 Pentonville Road
London N1 9JB, UK
and
400 Market Street, Suite 400
Philadelphia, PA 19106, USA

www.jkp.com

Library of Congress Cataloging in Publication Data
Robinson, Sally, 1969-
  Preventing the emotional abuse and neglect of people with intellectual disability
: stopping insult and injury / Sally Robinson ; foreword by Hilary Brown.
    pages cm
  ISBN 978-1-84905-230-6
  1. People with mental disabilities--Abuse of--Prevention. 2. People with mental
disabilities--Institutional care--Case studies. 3. People with mental disabilities-
-Services for. 4. Social work with people with mental disabilities. I. Title.
  HV3004.R63 2013
  362.3--dc23
                          2013014335

British Library Cataloguing in Publication Data
A CIP catalogue record for this book is available from the British Library

ISBN 978 1 84905 230 6
eISBN 978 0 85700 472 7

Printed and bound in Great Britain

A large debt of thanks is owed to the people who provided the foundations on which this book is built. The recollection and sharing of painful and difficult memories cannot have been an easy undertaking. I am grateful to each of the people who participated in the research for their agreement to be involved and the rigour with which they undertook the task.

This book is dedicated to Ann, Jim, Tom and Craig, their supporters Wendy, Gemma, Penny and Therese, and the family members Amanda, Datu, Ivy, Patrick and Rose, who participated on behalf of their much loved family members. While these are not your real names, they are most certainly your stories.

Contents

Foreword

This is a powerful account of the emotional abuse that people with intellectual disability have to endure and manage in their lives. Seeking to understand this abuse involves facing up to the cumulative damage it does to a person's self-esteem, eroding their confidence to move freely about their communities and negotiate their day-to-day relationships. Often we ascribe the 'problem' to the disabled person in these interactions when it is the acceptance and respect of the community that is at issue.

Nor should we evade responsibility by minimising these abuses. Whether we term them 'emotional abuse', 'teasing', 'bullying' or at the other end of the scale 'harassment' or 'hate crime' it seems as if we only have clumsy ways of addressing interactions that are nuanced and complicated. We need to be working to build bridges and create understanding, to heal these wounds and to create a truly non-discriminatory society, one where a person's horizons are not limited by the prejudices of others and where their aspirations are supported rather than undermined by the people they meet on their own particular journey.

The book also informs those involved in initiatives to counter abuse and to set in place proper arrangements between statutory agencies responsible for their different faces. The criminal justice system, the Public Guardian, government bodies, educators and social care services will all need to appreciate the impact of emotional abuse on individuals and their families. In taking action they will need to create robust structures that will not fail people at their most vulnerable times, while leaving with them a core of self-determination that allows them to make decisions about how to proceed wherever this is possible. This is never straightforward, as intimidation and harassment take their toll on a person's ability to think straight, whether or not that person is officially designated as someone who has an 'intellectual disability'. Feeling safe is central to the ability to make good choices about our relationships and our lives. Educators and counsellors will find this book a powerful place to start in addressing these issues with their students and clients.

Sally Robinson has documented these stories with respect and great care. Her methodology is meticulous, and she joins a tradition of international researchers committed to putting the voice of marginalised groups into the public domain. This is not a subject that can be understood through stand-alone statistics which often record and compare like with unlike, they zero in on those instances of abuse that are visible when so much is hidden or borne in silence. The figures can easily lose their context in a person's life history or in the gradual degradation of a relationship or escalating pattern of harm. Sometimes the figures lose a sense of proportion or fail to capture the double bind a person is in when they seek acceptance and inclusion only to be met with belittling and a new set of barriers at the hands of those they rely on. The figures are needed to inform service agencies, but they tell a very flat story.

Instead these stories are rich and the words of people with intellectual disability and their families do not only inform but they rightly haunt us, as fellow citizens and as a society. Those of us who advocate on behalf of people with intellectual disability, whether as relatives, carers, service managers, professionals, academics, or policy makers will do well to listen and take heed.

Hilary Brown
Professor of Social Care
Canterbury Christ Church University

Acknowledgements

I would like to thank Professors Lesley Chenoweth and Jayne Clapton for their keen interest, steadfast and insightful guidance and unflagging encouragement from the inception of the research to its conclusion. Additionally, thanks are due to the reference groups that provided advice to guide the research – both advocates and people with intellectual disability. The patient and thoughtful help of the editorial team at JKP is also much appreciated.

Finally, I would like to thank my family – Tony, Lucy and Caitlin – for their love and support.

Preface

The decision to write this book has been influenced by my experiences over the past 20 years as a disability service provider, individual and systemic advocate and researcher with people with disability. During this time, I have witnessed (and sometimes, it must be acknowledged, participated in) interactions that I now view to have been emotionally or psychologically abusive or neglectful. These may have been unintentionally abusive actions but when considered through the eyes of the person using the service, I have little doubt they were received as abusive.

During the last decade, I have had the opportunity to develop some close relationships with research colleagues who have intellectual disability, and over time we have become friends. They have spoken with me in some depth about their experiences of living in accommodation services in the past and about their experiences of what they consider emotional and psychological abuse and neglect.

I have reflected on these experiences with disquiet for several years, worried about the impact of this sort of abuse on people with intellectual disability, and been curious and concerned about why it has remained 'under the radar' in terms of recognition, response and policy in the disability accommodation and support sector.

This research grew from a suspicion that emotional and psychological abuse and neglect were happening often to many people with intellectual disability who live in accommodation services; that it was inadequately recognised; and that it was not responded to sufficiently well to either stop it or prevent it from happening. This book is not intended as a theoretical treatise on abuse but a living history of people's experience that paints a picture of the subtlety, the frequency and the impact of this form of abuse on the lives of people with intellectual disability and that makes an unapologetic call for change.

PART 1

Setting the Scene

There's so many different types of abuse, and it all comes down to the same thing. It's making people nothing. And Fran was nothing. There was never anything nice said about her, everything was negative. And she had to put up with that, and we had to put up with that, until we all sort of believed it, almost.

Amanda, Fran's mother

Chapter 1

Gaining New Understanding About Abuse Through the Lens of Lived Experience

This introductory chapter establishes the approach taken in this book; introduces its aims to provide a place for sharing the stories of people with intellectual disability about their experiences, to make change to policy and practice in disability services and to offer strategies and tools for capacity-building for practitioners; introduces the narrators of the stories and briefly describes the ways in which they came to contribute their stories to the book.

Why write a book like this?

The research that underpins this book is grounded in the belief that the insult, ignoring, belittling and humiliating that makes up a part of the 'service lives' of some people with intellectual disability is neither trivial nor forgettable. It is every bit as injurious as other forms of maltreatment. The words contained in the title of this book, *insult and injury*, give a clue that this work takes a perspectival approach to the experience of emotional and psychological abuse and neglect – that it is framed, as much as possible, through the eyes of those who have experienced it.

This study on which this book is based began from a premise that emotional and psychological abuse and neglect is an everyday occurrence in the lives of some people with intellectual disability who live in disability accommodation services. Interaction with a large number of staff, many of whom are casual workers, as well as co-residence with other people with disability who may have significant challenging behaviour and the depersonalising effects of group living all combine to make the likelihood of emotional and psychological abuse and neglect high for people living in these situations (Macfarlane 1994; Powers *et al.* 2002).

Little is known about emotional and psychological abuse and neglect in the lives of people with intellectual disability. Few people with intellectual disability have been asked about their experiences and their memories of this sort of abuse and neglect. The responses of still fewer have appeared in the research literature or influenced disability services policy.

The emotional and psychological abuse and neglect of people with intellectual disability in Australia remains largely un-investigated. Research with those who have experienced such abuse has not been conducted in Australia and is also under-investigated in an international context (O'Callaghan and Murphy 2003; Saxton 2009). A significant proportion of the existing research on the issue is situated either at a theoretical level or at an applied level, which, while important in developing our understanding of abuse, does not directly engage people with intellectual disability.

This book aims to share research about emotional and psychological abuse and neglect and – importantly – to use it to frame the narratives of nine people with intellectual disability who have experienced emotional and psychological abuse and neglect in their 'service lives'. Four people with intellectual disability shared their stories about longstanding abuse and neglect; a method called narrative collage was used to support them to build a montage of their experiences. Five family members also spoke about the abuse and neglect of their family members who have high support needs that precluded them from relating their own narratives. The resulting nine narratives, in which people share a disturbing and disquieting volume and range of harms, are the centrepiece of this book.

A series of new insights that have particular importance for policy and practice emerge from the lived experience of abuse of people with intellectual disability. These problems concern the central place of systems in this form of abuse and neglect; the cumulative impact of emotional and psychological abuse and neglect over time; recognition of emotional and psychological abuse and neglect *by* people with intellectual disability; and the lack of moral authority accorded to people with intellectual disability in abuse acknowledgement and reporting.

Structure of the book

The book is divided into three primary sections centred on the abuse narratives of people with intellectual disability, told by them and their families. Part 1 contextualises the emotional and psychological abuse and neglect of people with intellectual disability in terms of disability accommodation services and broader social and cultural relations. Part 2 of the book presents the narratives of people with intellectual disability and, in the case of people with high support needs, their family members. The perspectives of advocates, complaints agencies and policy makers are also represented here. Key issues of concern emerge from these stories of abuse and neglect, which offer insights into practice and policy and identify opportunities for change. Part 3 offers new insights from the research and strategies for building capacity and moving forward to make change in the lives of people with intellectual disability.

Looking through a particular lens

In reviewing the existing research about other abuse experiences (some including emotional and psychological abuse and neglect), it is clear that the views of people who have lived experience of abuse and neglect add a very meaningful depth and breadth to the understanding of abuse, which moves beyond physical domains and into the social and structural domains of society.

It is perhaps in part because we have begun to address sexual and physical abuse, inappropriate accommodation and the physical and social exclusion of people with disability (however incompletely) that more subtle and pervasive forms of abuse can be aired and given serious consideration. There is an unmistakable need to seek people's thoughts and views on their experiences of emotional and psychological abuse and neglect to extend this small but important body of work.

Why a narrative approach?

There is a history of excluding people with intellectual disability from directly participating in research on troublesome issues. A robust research literature exists on the involvement of people with disability in research that affects their lives. The shared contention of this work is that research is strengthened, both in terms of the quality and type of data obtained and the ethics of the study, when a participatory approach is used (Balcazar *et al.* 1998; Shakespeare 1997).

The holders of expert knowledge about emotional and psychological abuse and neglect are people who have the lived experience of the issue under question – people with intellectual disability and, for those people with high support needs, people who have supported them over long periods of time (family members, in this research).

At a more conceptual level, this research centres on the lived realities of people with intellectual disability and on the development of new ways of representing previously invalidating representations of people's lives. To do this it takes a perspectival position and takes a partisan, standpoint approach that privileges the participation and role of people with intellectual disability in the research and focuses on both their experiences of the phenomenon of abuse and neglect and also their strategies for dealing with it – what Lindemann Nelson (2001) calls the 'counterstories' they have developed to repair their damaged identities, or the tools of resistance they have used to avoid becoming victims.

Introducing the narrators

The brief descriptions that follow provide an introduction to each of the people who were involved in the research. Importantly, they also paint a picture of people as more than victims of abuse – this is critical to both people's self-conception and to the ontological approach of the research in its aim to confront the dominant negative conception of people with intellectual disability.

Ann, Jim, Tom and Craig provided a great deal of information about their experiences in our meetings together. Their narratives of the abuses they experienced living in a wide range of services are powerful and moving. The family members Ivy, Datu, Rose, Amanda and Patrick provided the information that forms the narratives of their family members – Jill, Diwata, Jenny, Fran and Dan. They were unable to participate in the study as they have high support needs due to their intellectual disability (or acquired brain injury in Dan's case). As will be seen, this perspective brings an added layer of concern and trauma to the experiences of harm of people with high support needs, which are profound and wide ranging.

All identifying details have been altered to protect the privacy of people who participated in the research – their names, the names of services and places they lived and the particular location in Australia in which the research took place. Further, each person has indicated their willingness to have their narratives included in the book.

Ann

Ann is in her early 40s, and lives alone in a small house. She enjoys being involved in craft and art groups, dancing, hydrotherapy and shopping. She receives individual support each day from a disability support service. Ann has been living here for about two years. She is a person who has intellectual disability, physical disability and psychiatric disability.

Before moving here, Ann spent the previous ten years living in a series of boarding houses and hostels,[1] a privately run group home, two nursing homes and two psychiatric institutions. She experienced a wide range of abuses in many of the facilities, including physical, sexual, emotional and psychological, chemical and financial abuse and neglect. Ann had an accident in a hostel and broke her hip, and finished up in a nursing home for a time, which appeared to be a catalyst for her leaving the boarding house sector. Her sister worked with an advocacy agency to find Ann her current support arrangement.

Tom

Tom lives with his dog in a social housing unit in a block of 12 units. He is happy with his unit but has a lot of trouble with his neighbours. He gets personal support each day from a new disability support service, which he is involved in managing. Tom is in his late 30s, and he has physical and intellectual disability.

Before he lived here Tom lived in many places, including in two large residential institutions, two group homes, at least three privately run hostels and on his own with paid support in three locations. He has had a wide range of good and bad experiences and is relishing the opportunity to be involved in managing the support that he now receives.

---

1   In Australia, boarding houses and hostels are unfunded privately operated facilities, which cater to people with and without disability. Hostels provide linen and meals and some assistance with laundry and medication.

Jim

Jim lives alone in a duplex unit in the suburbs, although his mum visits from the country now and again. He gets daily support from a large disability services organisation. Jim is in his early 40s, and he has intellectual disability and physical disability.

Jim has lived in residential care since he was a young child. He first moved out of his family home into a large residential institution at four years old and lived there until he was 18. After that he lived in several group homes and shared accommodation settings, before moving into his current home. He used to enjoy working in supported employment locally but after it closed down a couple of years ago he stays at home most days unless he's going shopping.

Craig

Craig lives in his own unit in the suburbs. He is a hardworking man in his mid 40s, who also is very involved with disability rights and giving talks to community groups. Craig has physical disability and was labelled as having intellectual disability in the past, although he's not sure that he in fact does.

Craig was placed in residential care as a baby. He lived in a residential institution throughout his childhood, leaving at 18. He then lived in several share arrangements before moving into his current home. Craig is Aboriginal, but was brought up not knowing this until he was a teenager.

Jill

Jill is a lady in her mid 40s, who lives alone in a small block of units. Her mother lives in a unit in the same complex and they spend a lot of time together. Jill and her mother, Ivy, have a very close and loving relationship.

Jill has very high support needs due to her intellectual disability and needs quite a lot of formal support. When she was 15 Jill moved into a large residential institution. She lived there for 17 years until moving into her current home ten years ago. Ivy says Jill experienced many abuses in the institution. Ivy knew about some of these at the time and others she found out about when she obtained Jill's file after Jill left the institution. Jill is not able to speak and so could not tell anyone about her experiences, good or bad. Ivy talks about times in the institution when Jill's health was very poorly managed and when she was seriously neglected.

Jill's experiences in the community have also been difficult, due to poorly trained service providers, ill-matched co-residents and under-resourcing. Her current situation works very well for her but at a substantial cost to Ivy, who, in her mid 70s, is spending at least 50 hours a week supporting Jill due to a shortfall in funding.

Dan

For half the week Dan shares his house with his brother, Patrick, and for the other half he shares with paid staff. He has been living here for 18 months. When he was 23 Dan had a football accident, which resulted in him acquiring a brain injury and physical disability. He is now in his mid 40s.

After his accident, Dan lived with his mum and dad for five years, until their health deteriorated. He then moved to a long-stay rehabilitation centre, where he lived for 14 years. Patrick says that Dan was not emotionally or psychologically sustained or nurtured at all while he lived in the centre and that he experienced a lot of abuse and neglect while he lived there.

Diwata

Diwata lives at home with her dad, Datu. She is currently an adult college student and enjoys spending time shopping and with her family, especially her nieces and nephews. Diwata has just turned 21 and she has intellectual disability. Diwata's family come from Thailand.

Diwata lived in residential care as a child, when she went to special school in a regional city away from her family. Her dad brought her home because she was so unhappy but this was hard because the service resisted. He feels that she had some abusive treatment while she was living in care.

Jenny

Jenny lives in the same house as another person with disability, although she has her own support workers. She has a close relationship with her mum, Rose, whom she sees regularly and is intimately involved in her life. Jenny is in her mid 20s and she has intellectual disability and epilepsy.

Jenny first lived in residential services when she was 14. Since then she has lived in a large hostel, then a group home, sharing with one other person. Her mother has been very active in seeking out innovative support options for Jenny.

Fran

Fran lives on her own in a house in the suburbs. She leads a busy life, going to several social activities and exercise classes during the week. Fran is 28 and she has autism and intellectual disability.

Fran moved into a large residential institution at the age of six. She stayed there until she was 18, when she moved into her current home. Her mother, Amanda, worked extremely hard to put together a support arrangement that she felt would support Fran well and that would allow her to live a decent life – something Amanda did not feel she had been able to do until then. Fran experienced a range of abuses when she was living in the institution and Amanda feels her life has changed dramatically since she moved into her own home and her family manages her support.

The diversity and range of experiences and perspectives of each of these people can be seen in depth in Chapter 4, where their recollections of abuse and neglect are described in detail. They are resilient and determined in the face of longstanding and often chronic harm, and it is important at the outset to acknowledge that this is not a book about victims but about people who have survived harms at many levels.

The next chapter focuses on understanding the context in which emotional and psychological abuse and neglect occur, discussing current research, policy and practice responses to this experience. A framework for defining and better understanding this form of abuse and neglect is laid out and explained, giving a detailed picture of some of the behaviours and interactions that make up this form of harm. Before moving into this domain a brief conversation should be had about the contested language and concepts in the multiple spaces of disability, emotional and psychological harm and abuse and neglect.

Shifting territory

The constructs 'emotional and psychological', 'abuse and neglect' and 'intellectual disability' are subject to ongoing and at times intense debate. Considerable heat and passion have been expended over the use and misuse of language, particularly around the way people with disability have been described – in both the past and present. It may be useful in this introductory chapter to clarify the rationale behind the way these particular central terms are used in this book.

There is an ongoing debate in the literature about the value of continuing to use the term 'abuse', as it may serve to undermine and diminish the seriousness of the violence and crimes that are committed against people with disability (Brown 2004; Sobsey 1994). Sexual and physical assault, theft, fraud, chemical restraint and false imprisonment are criminal acts and should be named and treated as such when they appear in the lives of people with disability. However, there may be some abuses that are not as clearly criminal wrongs (although they may in some cases be civil wrongs), which may still benefit from being conceived of as abuses of the rights of people with disability. These include emotional and psychological abuse and neglect, institutional abuse and systemic abuse.

Conway argues that the term 'abuse' draws on: 'ethical, sociological, psychological and philosophical understanding' (1994, p.15). A number of researchers talk about emotional and psychological abuse falling within a 'grey area' that is at the limits of legal behaviour, where the actions of the abuser are most certainly abusive but may not be criminal. In these situations, a more nuanced understanding or response may be needed – for example, how should we differentiate between a premeditated cruel action and one that was misguided but well intentioned, or one that was in compliance with service policy but a service policy that did not respect the human rights of the people living in the service? As will be demonstrated, the subtleties of action and effect that are at play in some emotional and psychological abuse and neglect demand a complex response, which requires a way of referring to this maltreatment that is broad enough to encompass moral, ethical and legal wrong (Clapton 2008b).

To make this even more complex, the language used by different authors to describe emotional and psychological abuse and neglect is inconsistent, both within and across fields of study. Emotional abuse, psychological abuse, psychological maltreatment, verbal abuse, systemic abuse, indirect abuse and non-physical contact abuse are all terms used in the literature to refer to a similar group of experiences. In this book, the terms 'emotional and psychological abuse' and 'neglect' are used. Emotional and psychological abuses are understood in this study to occupy different points on a continuum of harm.

There is also an ongoing debate regarding language to refer to people with disability. Language surrounding disability is strongly influenced by the debates concerning the social and political positioning of disability in sociological contexts. Social model theorists and researchers in the UK predominantly use the term 'disabled person' to acknowledge the fundamentally social, political and structural processes of disablement (Goodley 2003; Oliver and Barnes 1998). In Australia, this terminology does not have as strong a currency and 'person with disability' is more frequently used. This is also the usual preference of self-advocates, who prefer to be 'person first'. The terminology preferred by self-advocates in Australia, 'person with intellectual disability', is used in this book.

Chapter 2

What is This Harm?

This chapter develops themes relevant to understanding the context in which this abuse and neglect occurs. It provides a background to the stories, canvasses other research about abuse and neglect and presents and explains the framework of emotional and psychological abuse and neglect.

What is this harm?

As we will see, defining this form of harm is not an easy endeavour. Emotional and psychological abuse and neglect are difficult and complex to define and remain a source of debate in the literature for many reasons.

- It is undoubtedly harder to identify than other forms of mistreatment.

- No injury can be seen, unless the person has also undergone physical or sexual assault.

- The impact of emotional and psychological abuse, while it can be severe, may be cumulative, reliant on a sustained attack on the person's psyche.

- Unlike sexual or physical assault, emotional and psychological abuse may be unintentional on the part of the abuser (as in the case of a staff member following an unnecessarily restrictive behaviour management plan).

- It is difficult to isolate from other forms of abuse because other forms of abuse also include emotional or psychological harm.

- Some authors argue that it is more strongly associated with the domain of omission whereas most other forms of abuse and assault reside within the domain of commission or action – so neglect may have a more complex role to play than in other abuse areas. (Iwaniec, Larkin and Higgins 2006; McKinnon 2008; Penhale 1999; Sobsey 1994)

Emotional and psychological abuse is poorly recognised and responded to in the lives of people with intellectual disability in research and in policy, apart from the small number of studies that directly ask people with disability about their experiences, where it features strongly as a common experience. It is rarely seen as what Macfarlane describes as: 'subtle abuse in its often monotonous and sometimes threatening and cunning forms' (1994, p.88). Few studies give attention to recovery, resistance and resilience of people with disability in the face of this abuse and neglect. Government and service policy frameworks in several countries give little attention to addressing this form of abuse and neglect and there are few avenues of legal redress for people who have suffered it.

Emotional and psychological abuse and neglect are experienced by people with intellectual disability living in supported accommodation services in many and varied ways:

- as a single incident
- as a pattern of behaviour (or an abusive relationship) from one individual abuser
- as the failure of an individual to provide essential emotional care
- as a series of single incidents carried out by a number of individuals
- as a series of patterns of behaviour (or abusive relationships) from a number of individuals at the same time
- as part of a behaviour management plan or treatment plan
- as a lifestyle caused by institutional routines and frameworks that influence the conduct of management, staff and/or other residents. (Brown 2007; Horne, Merz and Merz 2001; Ticoll 1995)

Definitions of emotional and psychological abuse

Women With Disabilities Australia, in its global review of violence against women with disabilities, draws from the work of many researchers to define emotional or psychological violence as:

> the infliction of anguish, pain, or distress through verbal or non-verbal acts and/or behaviour. It results in harm to a person's self-concept and mental well-being as a result of being subjected to behaviours such as verbal abuse, continual rejection, withdrawal of affection, physical or social isolation and harassment, or intimidation. (2007, p.33)

Other definitions in the disability abuse literature include reference to lack of love and affection, corrupting, belittling, threats, verbal attacks, taunting and shouting that leads to the victim's loss of confidence and self-esteem and omissions of care that produce harm. Saxton takes an interesting approach and rejects an incident-based notion of abuse. She and her colleagues at the World Institute on Disability state: 'We regard abuse as a continuum of systematic mistreatment, extreme or subtle, the visible version of disability oppression' (2009, pp.3–4).

Nosek *et al.* define emotional abuse in their study as: 'being threatened, terrorised, corrupted, or severely rejected, isolated, ignored or verbally attacked' (2001a, p.180). Ticoll (1994) writes at length about features of emotional and psychological abuse that have particular resonance in the lives of people with disability. These include threats by attendant care workers, threats by social workers to remove children, threats of institutionalisation, verbal taunts from neighbours or strangers on the street and lack of respect by caregivers. Ticoll quotes a respondent in their study as saying: 'the climate of insult is present all the time, everyday' (1994, p.13).

Emotional and psychological neglect

Sobsey is one of the few writers who specifically discuss emotional neglect in the literature. He states that:

> Neglect is perhaps the most insidious form of abuse; in extreme form it may be one of the most damaging… Emotional or developmental neglect occurs when an individual is deprived of basic human interactions required for the development of normal behaviour. (1994, p.34)

Jenkins and Davies (2006) argue that abuse literature has not fully engaged with a broader definition of neglect. Their research found that because acts of neglect stem from the activities of daily living, they are less likely to be seen by visitors or inspectors. As well, they found practitioners to have a different attitude towards neglect and a far lower recognition of it.

Prevalence

There is little attempt to assess the prevalence of emotional and psychological abuse and neglect in the abuse literature. In any case, as will be discussed below, there are two considerably different positions on the prevalence of this form of abuse, which makes any estimate extremely difficult.

Few studies give active consideration to the experience of emotional and psychological abuse and neglect. While most include them in the range of abuses experienced by people, they do not feature in discussion. Those writers who do give consideration to emotional and psychological abuse and neglect take two positions. The first assumes that the experience of emotional and psychological abuse is a separable category of abuse, and thus several studies cite figures for the experience of this form of abuse as a discrete phenomenon among people with a range of disabilities (e.g., Nosek *et al.* 2001; Saxton *et al.* 2001). The second, more dominant position states that as well as occurring on its own, emotional and psychological abuse underpins most other forms of abuse and so is considerably more prevalent than has been recognised (Brown 1999; Conway 1994). Sobsey notes:

> Psychological abuse is the most complex form of abuse to objectively define or detect. It is also difficult to isolate from other forms of abuse because sexual abuse, neglect and even physical abuse all produce psychological harm, which can be the most devastating of all consequences. (1994, p.33)

This is consistent with the literature from the child, elder and women's abuse fields. As well as being experienced as the sole form of abuse, emotional and psychological abuse is a *precondition* for a range of other mistreatments.

This study also draws from a body of work on the abuse of adults with intellectual disability that, while figures vary widely, is consistent in the assertion that all forms of abuse are experienced by many, or even most, people living in formal disability services (Conway, Bergin and Thornton 1996; McCarthy and Thompson 1996; Sobsey 1994; Ticoll 1994). Obtaining figures on the prevalence of abuse and neglect of people with disability, and people with intellectual disability, is problematic – studies use different methodologies, sampling and definitions, making comparison difficult. No reliable prevalence figures are available. However, several researchers comment on a range of studies that show that people with disability are subjected to considerably higher rates of abuse and neglect than people without disability. Figures range widely, but all point to a much higher than average experience of physical, sexual and financial abuses. While some figures are available, the ranges between studies are so wide as to make comparison of very limited benefit. For this reason, figures are not included in this book.

Horne *et al.* (2001) analyse the mental health consequences and social implications of the emotional and psychological abuse of people with disability. They contend that the prevalence of emotional abuse of people with disability is such that the impact of the trauma experienced by individuals also becomes part of a more widespread embedded social trauma. This is manifested through social and cultural practices that are largely unrecognised as potentially abusive, including those that have traditionally stigmatised and marginalised people with disability, such as institutionalisation, segregation and isolation. This social trauma is addressed through social repression and denial, which allow abusive social and cultural practices to continue. Horne *et al.* call for an increased social focus on the causes, rather than the symptomology of abuse and increased recognition of the impact of stigmatisation and marginalisation.

Why is this happening?

There are a range of theoretical understandings of the social, cultural and structural roles and places of people with intellectual disability. They share several features, most notably to do with the oppression, isolation and dehumanising of people with intellectual disability – all forces that substantially increase the conditions under which emotional and psychological abuse is likely to occur and recur.

'Othering' and humanness

Social constructionists argue that the abuse of people with intellectual disability continues due to their extreme marginalisation and their positioning as 'other' or less human – that they have been categorised through cultural practices as being somehow fit for treatment that would be deemed inappropriate for someone without an intellectual disability (Clapton 2008b; Taylor and Bogdan 1989). Lanoix (2005) claims that care is commodified in institutional environments and that this objectifies the resident as a set of needs. This gives rise to a climate of 'moral laissez faire' in which abuse more easily occurs. Chenoweth writes:

> The capacity of institutions and service systems to dehumanise is a powerful precursor to cultures of institutional violence. This construction of the victim as non-human occurs in subtle yet powerful ways... Once a person is dehumanised in this way, the usual constraints on abuse and violence become weakened and people are more likely to be verbally abused, beaten, sexually abused, tied up or locked up. (1995, p.40)

Nunkoosing (2000) holds that some explanations about intellectual disability are privileged over others – namely, that the knowledge of professionals and academics is privileged over that of people with intellectual disability themselves. In the context of abuse, the consequence of this is that the lived experience of the subtleties of emotional and psychological abuse by people with intellectual disability have been largely ignored in favour of the privileged professional explanations of abuse, which focus predominantly on sexual and physical abuse.

Identity constructions – damaged identities

Lindemann Nelson's (2001) work around damaged identities and narrative repair is used as an ontological foundation for this research and it is also important in understanding the damage that is done to the identity of people with intellectual disability through emotional and psychological abuse. Lindemann Nelson holds that personal identity is a lever that expands or contracts a person's ability to exercise moral agency, according to the way in which they are identified by others and the way in which they identify themselves. In the case of people who are identified by others as morally defective or lacking, certain actions are perceived as being appropriate or permissible that would not be so for people who are not so labelled, such as hospitalisation, humouring or being treated with contempt or hostility – or being abused. Not only are actions available to others, but the self-identification of people as morally defective or lacking means they will mistrust their own capabilities and treat themselves with suspicion or contempt or exempt themselves from full responsibility for their actions, thus restricting their own moral agency.

Where an entire group is identified as morally defective or lacking (as in the case of people with intellectual disability), Lindemann Nelson talks of the construction of mandatory identities, where social expectations are set up about how group members are expected to behave, what they can know, what can be demanded of them and to whom they are answerable. This is what she calls damaged identities. Individual identities are subsumed into a marginalised social group experience.

In the context of emotional and psychological abuse and neglect of people with intellectual disability, a morally compromised identity is constructed and maintained for service users by service management (through policies that fail to adequately engage people's human rights), service workers (through work practices that inadequately humanise people with disability) and people with intellectual disability themselves. This identity is likely to increase the risk of abuse occurring significantly and may also contribute to the creation of a climate in which the response to such abuse is likely to be less than vigorous or rigorous, due to the increased vulnerabilities and decreased lack of protections accorded to people who are socially identified as service users.

Nelson also argues that because identities are constructed and damaged narratively, they can also therefore be repaired through narrative means. This is done through the counterstory – a narrative that develops group members as fully developed moral agents. The counterstory is designed to act in two ways. First, in altering the perception of the dominant group of the subgroup and assisting them to see the subgroup as worthy of moral respect. Second, the counterstory aims to alter the person's self-perception and increase their resilience.

Exclusionary ethics

The normative ethics that have been applied to people with intellectual disability in relation to their experience of abuse and neglect have resulted in institutional practices in which abuse is not seen for what it is; where the abrading of the rights and dignity of people who use services is unrecognised; and where the usual moral concerns applied to other community members are suspended. It allows for the 'othering' of people with intellectual disability, the creation of what Clapton (2008b) terms a 'discourse of disqualification', in which people with intellectual disability are exempted from prevailing ethical considerations or perspectives and the profound exclusion that results.

Spatial and social constructions
– 'keeping people in their place'

Social geographers Kitchin (1998) and Hall (2004) argue that both spaces and social relations are organised to keep people with disability 'in their place' and to convey to people with disability that they are 'out of place' (Kitchin 1998). According to this view, disability is spatially as well as socially constructed and the rules that operate on a tacit as well as an overt level form structures that guide the operation of social and cultural practices. Kitchin states: 'These structures form, sustain and perpetuate the popular stereotypes which underlie many exclusionary practices and are enshrined within the maintenance of the dominant ideology' (1998, p.352).

Hall (2004) contends that the social inclusion agenda has inadvertently excluded people with intellectual disability by establishing criteria for inclusion to which they either cannot or do not want to aspire, while at the same time marginalising the spaces and roles that they filled before the social inclusion agenda began. This leaves people with intellectual disability almost stateless – not included, yet not left behind – and they are left particularly open to discrimination, rejection and abuse by individuals, groups and institutions.

The constructions of people with intellectual disability as 'other', as damaged, as less than human and as needing to be 'kept in their place' are powerful and dominant modes of social and cultural operation and they have informed the development of the structures, including the disability services systems, within which people live today. As such, these constructions have direct relevance to this research and to understanding the impact of emotional and psychological abuse and neglect in the lives of people with intellectual disability.

What does this mean in the lives of people with intellectual disability?

A key to the way in which abuse and neglect of people with disability is viewed and responded to lies in the way shared understandings of disability are operationalised. The conceptions of disability that underpin the development and application of disability service models directly influence the way in which abuse and neglect are understood and responded to and the degree to which people are protected from its occurrence. The three primary models that have predominantly influenced provision of accommodation support to people with disability over time can be presented as follows:

1. The medical model/welfare model – in which disability is a problem that is located within the individual, best responded to with appropriate treatment by trained professionals (Harrison 2000).

2. Normalisation/social role valorisation – in which the focus is on making available to people with intellectual disability the same patterns and conditions of everyday life in the same way as they are available to other members of the community (Perrin 1999).

3. The social model/social approaches – social constructs that distinguish between impairment and disability and see society as a primary causative factor in disability, due to the ways in which it oppresses disabled people (Tregaskis 2002).

However, in practice, there are still many areas where the medical, or 'personal tragedy', and the welfare models of disability (where disability is seen to be a 'problem' that is located within the individual) are paramount in both the design and the implementation of services and social structures (MacArthur 2003). When this is the case, services are welfare oriented or medicalised in approach and seek to treat the symptom of the person's lack of access or inclusion rather than to change the root cause of the problem. This leaves people with impairments as the recipients of specialist services, rather than included through universal design principles and inclusive policies and practices. In the case of abuse and neglect within disability services, this results in common responses that aim to protect clients and address individual instances of abuse, but that arguably fail to consider abuse and neglect as a phenomenon affecting a whole population group, which is driven and influenced by complex social, cultural and political forces (Brown 2004; Marsland, Oakes and White 2007).

While the conceptions of disability that shape the dominant social, structural and policy responses to people with intellectual disability in Australia have changed significantly over the past few decades, in many instances people with intellectual disability are still viewed as non-gendered, non-powerful non-citizens (Goggin and Newell 2005; Sherry 1999), particularly inside the disability services framework. It is also important to note, as Brown identifies, that: 'Although it is tempting to characterise the history of services as one long progression, all of these strands are recognisable within our current service systems' (1994, p.128).

When there is a broad social acceptance of a group having less access to their rights and having difficulty in having those rights upheld, systems are seemingly allowed to develop that, mostly unintentionally, allow emotional and psychological abuse to thrive.

Vulnerability and risk

There are both individual and systemic factors that influence how vulnerable a person is to abuse and neglect. People with intellectual disability are not vulnerable by virtue of having intellectual disability – it is other factors in their lives, such as the reliance on others to meet physical care needs, impairments that limit a person's ability to recognise abuse or residence in institutional settings that may make them so (Nosek *et al.* 2001a; Sobsey 1994). The structural, social and political circumstances that surround community and society responses to people with disability in large part determine and increase the vulnerability of people with intellectual disability to abuse. These include poverty, unemployment and underemployment, inadequate housing, poor-quality health care, exposure to domestic violence and social stereotypes of vulnerability (Fawcett 2008; Women With Disabilities Australia 2007).

Exposure to large numbers of casual and agency staff, lack of control over which staff provide intimate care services, lack of control generally over day-to-day decisions and larger life decisions, organisational structures that focus strongly on systems management rather than individual support, poverty, unemployment and underemployment, lack of access to essential services, stigma and marginalisation and discrimination all combine to increase the vulnerability and isolation of people with disability who live in disability accommodation services (Horne *et al.* 2001; White *et al.* 2003). These factors may have a far more insidious and far reaching effect on vulnerability, and the way in which we respond to vulnerability, than does, for instance, a physical reliance on care or an intellectual reliance on support to manage finances.

Research by Marsland *et al.* (2007) sought to identify aspects of intellectual disability service cultures and environments that could act as early indicators that people with intellectual disability were at risk of abuse. They found that the behaviours, actions, attitudes and decisions of managers and staff, the behaviours of people with intellectual disability, isolation, service design, placement planning and commissioning and fundamental care and the quality of the environment were all critical in preventing a climate in which abuse could flourish.

The impact of power relations

Marsland *et al.* also found that power, choice and the organisational climate were significant issues, noting that:

> power is a significant construct underlying the issue of abuse. Specific issues relating to power have been associated with cultures of abuse. Where there are imbalances of power at any level within the care hierarchy, there is a risk that power will be used inappropriately, increasing the risk of abuse. (2007, p.12)

It is argued that there is a serious imbalance of power structured into traditional disability services, which perpetuates a climate that is ripe for abuse. Mandeville and Hanson contend that this power imbalance is pervasive and that it: 'permeates program policy, agency culture, professional practice, and the personal dynamics in paid relationships' (2000, p.15). Ticoll (1994) details some of the ways in which people with disability are less powerful than those who abuse them. In some situations people are reliant on perpetrators for physical, psychological or economic support or other necessities; they do not have control over the actions of others who have the potential to invade or disrupt their lives or wellbeing; and they lack credibility or 'voice' if they have the opportunity to make a complaint about their mistreatment.

According to the seminal work of Wardhaugh and Wilding on the corruption of care (1993), a number of organisational factors are in play that result in the conception of people using services as less than fully human – including the neutralisation of normal moral concerns, isolation, a failure of management and lack of accountability and an enclosure of the organisation from scrutiny. Failure to address the fundamental imbalance of power leaves people with intellectual disability vulnerable to the potential abuse of individuals and systems, as they have little recourse to change their own situations.

The place of institutional abuse

Institutional abuse is important in extending the understanding of the range and scope of behaviours that happen within the experience of emotional and psychological abuse and neglect, given that it focuses explicitly on people's experiences in formal environments of care. Institutional abuse appears to have first been expressed as a serious issue of concern for people with disability in the early 1990s. Two conceptions of institutional abuse have arisen. The first centres on place – the institution itself. The second centres on practices and cultures.

Sobsey defines institutional abuse as the: 'neglectful, psychological, physical or sexual abuse that takes place in the managed institutional care of human beings' (1994, p.90). He also contends that abuse in group homes and other community-based supported accommodation environments should be considered institutional abuse if the nature of the relationship between the person being abused and the abuser is determined, at least in part, by the service system. For Sobsey, there are four factors that make institutional abuse unique:

1. extreme power inequities between residents and staff

2. the collective nature of the abuse

3. the abuse is covered up or the knowledge of it is not shared outside the institutions

4. there are clearly defined patterns of environmental influence.

Brown understands institutional abuse to be: 'not really a "type" of abuse, or even just a "site" of abuse, but a constellation of factors that interact to produce poor care, insensitive practice and to either provoke or condone individual or collective acts of cruelty' (2007, p.2).

The sorts of practices that occur within this conception of institutional abuse include the development and maintenance of poor-quality environments, oppressive routines, neglect of the needs, preferences and aspirations of people living in the service, practices that are outside of community norms, individual and group cruelty and negligence.

Gender and abuse

It is also important that analyses of violence and abuse do not overlook the importance of gender. Much of the literature on violence and disability concerns women with disability (see, for example, Chenoweth 1996; Howe 2000; Women With Disabilities Australia 2007). It is important, however, to also consider the disempowered position of men with intellectual disability in disability services, particularly in their relationships with staff and management of those services.

The literature on emotional and psychological abuse of people with disability pays less attention to gender than does the literature and research on sexual and physical abuse. This may be because the material has a stronger concentration on abuse occurring within institutional and service-oriented contexts, and thus people with disability are conceived more in the role of 'clients' or 'residents' than 'men' or 'women'.

While gender is both relevant and important to any analysis of violence and abuse, it is overly simplistic to argue that one gender is more disempowered, or more discriminated against than another in this context. Both men and women with intellectual disability are marginalised and isolated in disability accommodation services and both are potentially victimised by emotional and psychological abuse and neglect. The technologies of that abuse may be different for women and men – there simply does not appear to be research that has considered this to date, indicating a need for studies that address these issues.

Models for understanding abuse and neglect

Models that explain the multiple dynamics underpinning abuse and neglect can be helpful in understanding why this harm continues in the lives of people with intellectual disability, despite ongoing attempts to prevent it.

Several researchers present models of abuse that seek to understand the complex factors at play and go beyond the 'bad apple' conception of a single abuser who is acting out of malevolent intent within an otherwise wholly safe environment. These approaches share a view that there are multiple strata in which the preconditions for abuse are laid.

Penhale (1999) distinguishes three levels of institutional abuse:

1. between individuals within the residential setting

2. abuse that arises due to the operational regime of the institution

3. abuse that arises at a system level, caused by the broader structure of society.

Penhale, in her work in the elder abuse field (Bennett, Kingston and Penhale 1997), also talks of abuse as existing at three different structural levels:

1. the macro (political) level

2. the mezzo (institutional) strata

3. the micro (individual) level.

An alternative view is presented by Sobsey, who develops an integrated ecological model of abuse (1994) that draws from the work of Bronfenbrenner in the child abuse field. In essence, the model describes the interaction of culture, environment and relationships as core factors in the occurrence of abuse. His contention is that abusive incidents and relationships are influenced and made possible by power inequities, the modelling of abusive relations, the minimisation of counter-controls and, at the broadest cultural level, the provision of a rationale for power inequities in the lives of people with disability.

A third approach to understanding abuse is presented by Brown, who identifies three different frameworks for understanding abuse, according to the type of harm done; the relationship between the perpetrator and the client and/or their gender or position; and the context in which it occurs and the systems that need to be engaged to deal with it. In this last typology, Brown divides abuse into several categories, including ordinary crime; inequitable access to basic services due to discrimination; ethical dilemmas; deliberate and predatory abuse; and: 'abuses which arise out of professional or service relationships in which unequal power, institutional dynamics, poor training and low expectations conspire to produce rigid, depersonalising environments and callous or ignorant individual responses' (2004, p.41–42).

This understanding of abuse is potentially very useful in seeking to understand emotional and psychological abuse and neglect of people with intellectual disability who live in disability accommodation services. However, abuse that has an institutional cause may be experienced by the individual in the same way as abuse that has a predatory cause – the behaviour of staff may be the same in the case of emotional and psychological abuse, where the person is ignored, degraded or harassed. It may be also be difficult to know in many cases, particularly where the person does not have conventional speech, whether the abuse they have experienced is institutional/systemic in nature or a result of the deliberate targeting of an individual person.

Each of the models presented here shares the assertion that abuse occurs on multiple levels, in multiple contexts and in interrelated ways. It is therefore a far more complex experience than can be adequately represented in a linear policy and procedural response to isolated incidents of abuse or neglect, so frequently used in disability services.

Building our understanding of emotional and psychological abuse and neglect

In this section of the book, we will build a picture of what the existing research with people with intellectual disability and other groups of people who experience high rates of abuse can tell us about the experience of emotional and psychological abuse and neglect.

What have people with intellectual disability already told us about their experiences of this harm?

There are already a limited number of studies that directly ask people with intellectual disability about their abuse experiences. This work paints a clear picture of emotional and psychological abuse as a common experience in the lives of people with intellectual disability – so common that researchers reported it was not recognised by many people who participated in research to be out of the ordinary. While small, this is an important body of research to connect with this book as a developing history.

All of these studies clearly demonstrate that emotional and psychological abuse and neglect have a significant negative impact on the lives of people with intellectual disability, even when people are unable to name the abuse for what it is. These studies discuss with people with intellectual disability their perceptions of abuse in broader frameworks than the more common paradigms of sexual and physical abuses.

For example, in the institutional context Malacrida asked 21 people with intellectual disability about their experiences of a time-out room in an institution for 'mental defectives' in the UK. Using a standpoint epistemology and a narrative methodology, she found what she terms: 'a profoundly convincing personal and political argument against the institution's routine and systemic violence, and ultimately, against institutionalisation itself' (2005, p.535).

She notes that for most participants in the research, discussing their experiences was seen as an upsetting, but: 'necessary and important political and personal act' (2005, p.524). People who participated in the research told of being humiliated, demeaned, physically assaulted, and dehumanised by staff in the process of being contained in the time-out room of the institution.

Sequiera and Halstead reviewed the few studies that have included the views of people with intellectual disability about restraint and seclusion. They note that service users report strong negative feelings about restraint and seclusion, that it worsens their mental state, that it re-traumatises people with a history of abuse or rape and that:

> they perceived those who are executing the physical intervention to be malevolent; as using the restraint to control or punish, as using unnecessary force or using physical intervention in an arbitrary way...[and] to be laughing or enjoying the experience. (2002, p.19)

Jones and Stenfert Krose (2006) also studied the views of service users with intellectual disability about physical restraint procedures in secure settings. They interviewed ten people in depth and report more mixed findings than Sequiera and Halstead. They were surprised to find an absence of emotional content in people's responses to the questions, given the topic, and put this down to the routine place that restraint had in their lives. Participants had mixed views on whether staff enjoyed restraining them, and two participants described abusive practices. The authors caution that there may be a tendency for people with intellectual disability to be overly generous about the service they receive and to acquiesce to questions asked, hence a need to take care in wording questions – they identify one of their questions as overly leading and possibly contributing to the unexpectedly positive findings of the study.

These studies highlight the importance of problematising the responses of staff and services to the 'challenging behaviour' that abused people may use to deal with the emotions called up by their experiences. Challenging behaviour is the term currently used in policy to describe behaviour used by people with disability that has the potential to harm themselves and those around them or to impact significantly on their access to the community. It does, however, need to be acknowledged as a term of policy and service systems, not the language of people with disability.

Taking a broader approach to understanding abuse, The Roeher Institute conducted a large study in Canada with people with a range of disabilities, including people with intellectual disability. A narrative approach was taken, in order to tease out concerns that stories The Institute was hearing from people with disability did not reflect the definitions of abuse that were in common use in Canada. The aim of the study was to give people with disability a voice in naming violence and abuse. When people with disability were interviewed in depth about their understanding of violence and abuse, the impact of it on their lives and how it made them feel, the researchers found that:

> From that perspective, violence and abuse look somewhat different. In the experience of those with disabilities, it is not only the traditional acts of hitting, sexually assaulting or verbally abusing a person that are defined as violent. It is, in fact, a wide gamut of actions or lack of actions that create suffering or trauma. It is being pulled into an uncomfortable position. It is being isolated at home and not being allowed to go to school. It is being forced to eat food or being denied food. It is being given medication that takes away one's sense of control. It is being left sitting on the toilet for long periods of time. (1995, p.ix)

Saxton *et al.* conducted a study with 72 women with physical and intellectual disability in the USA about their perceptions of abuse they had experienced from personal assistance providers, both formal and informal. Only seven of these women had intellectual disability. The researchers found that the personal assistance relationship being carried out in the women's homes was complex and boundaries were difficult for women to define and maintain, particularly around personal care. Overall, emotional abuse was the most highly reported form of abuse, taking forms including yelling and screaming, threats of abandonment, being ignored, threats to neglect children or pets and violations of privacy. The authors report that the focus group approach provided a learning opportunity for many women, as the majority of participants did not recognise and define their own and other women's experiences as abusive before discussing them with others. They state: 'The often subtle nature of the abuse resulted in women wondering if what they had experienced was intentional or unintentional' (2001, p.404).

Issues of recognition of abuse were also addressed by Collier *et al.* in a study where the authors worked with 26 people who use augmentative communication to address protective factors against sexual abuse. They found that while not all participants reported abuses, most of them expressed that they had: 'experienced or continued to experience a range of indignities and abuses in their lives' (2006, p.67). As with Saxton's study, Collier and colleagues found that many of the people who participated in their study did not recognise abusive treatment to be so until they discussed it with others. They cite many instances of emotional and psychological abuse, including being threatened with the withdrawal of services; being subjected to degrading comments; being given the 'silent treatment' from their service providers and caregivers; being denied the right to personal autonomy and decision-making by service providers; and not being allowed to communicate by service providers.

Two studies were located that aimed to assess the traumatic impact of abuse on people with intellectual disability. O'Callaghan and Murphy (2003) included people with severe intellectual disability and their families in a study to measure post traumatic stress disorder in people who had experienced abuse. Mitchell, Clegg and Furniss (2006) also interviewed people with intellectual disability to assess post traumatic stress disorder. Both of these studies found that the consequences for survivors of abuse were profound and long lasting.

While not including people with intellectual disability, two other works should be mentioned here, due to their similarity in approach to this study. Using a heuristic life narrative approach, Fitzerman's doctoral thesis explored the experience of abuse with people with physical disability. Her central finding was that:

> Subtle and emotional forms of abuse were experienced as common characteristics in everyday life. These forms of abuse were indicated to be represented by non-contact and contact form. Such acts were generally perceived as of a long duration, endemic in: social, familial, institutional and interpersonal constructs and detrimental to participants life's [sic] circumstances. The implications of such abuse was seen to undermine their emotional and personal integrity, personal rights and self determination. (1999, p.1)

Saxton, in her recent edited collection of narratives by people with disability about their experiences of abuse and neglect (2009), expresses concern that the internalising of messages of invalidation and powerlessness are one of the most insidious and little recognised aspects of abuse. These internalised messages not only impact on the self-esteem and self-worth of people but also open the door to further abuse.

There is a small but important literature that focuses on the resilience of people with intellectual disability in the face of maltreatment. Stefansdottir and Traustadottir present the stories of three women with intellectual disability who participated in a women's history group, during which they talked about their experiences of living in a residential institution for people with disability. They found all three women actively used a variety of strategies to cope with their experiences of institutionalisation and: 'fought to hold on to their human dignity, independence and sense of self-worth' (2006, p.66). Many times, these actions were interpreted by others as behaviour problems. The authors conclude that:

> People with learning difficulties have historically been cast into many negative roles such as the role of the helpless eternal child or, even worse, as not human. It is therefore hard for many to relate to their common humanity and recognise their acts of resistance and resilience, even when it is openly expressed. (2006, p.66)

It is clear that the views of people with intellectual disability in research add a very meaningful depth and breadth to the understanding of abuse that moves beyond physical domains and into the social and structural domains of society. An unmistakable need can be seen for research that explicitly seeks their thoughts and views on their experiences of emotional and psychological abuse and neglect to extend this small but important body of work.

Autobiographies by people with disability about emotional and psychological abuse and neglect

There is a small but growing Australian body of work by people with disability, or people close to them, about their experiences of living in disability accommodation services, including their experiences of emotional and psychological abuse and neglect. These autobiographies are often hard to find as they are frequently self-published or published in small numbers – despite the absorbing stories contained within their pages they do not seem to have yet attracted a mainstream audience. The collaboration between Dorothy Atkinson and Mabel Cooper to share her life story (Atkinson 2010) is perhaps the best known example of this genre and Trinity College in Dublin also share many fine stories through their 'A story to tell' project (Hughes 2011). However, due to the difficulty in locating autobiographies, this book shares only Australian stories.

The autobiographies of people with intellectual disability are harder to locate than those of people with other disabilities. This may be because it is more difficult for people with intellectual disability to write their autobiography without a co-author, which brings with it a whole host of issues about ownership, financial capacity and time. A number of what Atkinson and Walmsley (1999) call 'autobiographical fragments' were located. They are told in myriad ways – Robert Strike tells his story to a journalist in the mainstream media as an ambassador for an international day of people with disability (Bradley 2008), Doug Pentland tells his life history to a co-author and together they write a book (Pentland and Cincotta 1995), Jane tells her story through video (Smith and Ward 2007) and Robert Martin shares some of his past experiences as part of a conference plenary paper (2006a), which then forms the foundations of a journal article (2006b) and is also used in lobbying for the UN Convention on the Rights of Persons with Disabilities.

All of these stories share similar themes of isolation, oppression and lack of control over both minor and major areas of life when abuse happens. Each of the authors is looking back on their abuse experiences from a position of relative safety and power as respected self-advocates and community members and through a lens of time passed. Some of the authors recognise emotional abuse. Robert Martin, for instance, says in his conference presentation that: 'the emotional abuse was the worst kind of all' (2006a). Others understand abuse in more concrete terms and talk about the bad treatment they received and its lasting impact.

For example, Jane's video story contrasts life now with life in an institution and a community residential unit (in Smith and Ward 2007). She tells of her early service experiences:

> It was like a gaol, it was. And the nurses punished us, they did. And the punishment we got from the nurses, if we like wet ourselves or if we done something that we weren't supposed to, the nurses would punish us and tell us to go in the corner, they would. Or go to bed early, they would, or go without food. Yes, sometimes I feel like swearing, do you know what I mean, when it comes back? It brings back bad memories, it does. Good memories, sometimes, when you used to get away with things, not get caught.

Robert Strike, in describing his life in an institution for people with intellectual disability to a journalist for a major newspaper (Bradley 2008, p.15), says:

> It was tough, it was rough. When I was young I just watched people. I kept my mouth shut a lot, I was punished a lot, I was tied in a chair a lot 'cause I had a big mouth.

Autobiographies by people with a range of other disabilities are also included here and feature similarly abusive experiences. Without exception, all of the authors describe experiences of abuse and neglect in residential care. These experiences have had a significant impact on each of their lives. In all of their works, the authors talk about the subtle, monotonous abuses of their rights, which rob them of their autonomy and their dignity but don't breach the law. Several authors are repeatedly punished for complaining about these abuses. Meriel Stanger writes:

> One particular nurse smacked me on my bottom for wetting the bed. I reported this nurse to the head of nursing in that department. The nurse later sought me out and gave me a hard time. I learnt after that. Make the complaint after you leave, not while you are still living there. (2004, p.56)

Jan Daisley has published a two-volume autobiography (2005, 2007). She chronicles time spent in a large residential institution, after a catastrophic surgical accident left her with severe physical impairments, and then her move into the community into a series of group homes. Jan details a dismaying range of emotional, physical and financial abuses in her books. Many of these are the 'drip, drip, drip' of systemic abuse – staff who fail to turn up on time, or fail to turn up at all; rough handling; and disrespectful comments. Jan's ferocious drive and intellect – she completes two university degrees, sits on several boards of management and is politically active – do not appear to protect her from these experiences. After having had two toes broken by a staff member pushing her shower chair into the doorjamb, and being told 'not to be a wuss' (p.247), Jan writes:

> people believe I can cope with anything, which is a load of hogwash. I am like every other human being with feelings and emotions, but to some, my dependence on a wheelchair and other people, negates my human life and my ability to feel pain – likewise my psychological capacity to handle the disempowerment, let alone recognise it, which is one of my biggest bugbears... I had to be very careful with all I said and did in case I was labelled as having a behaviour problem again. (2007, p.248)

There have been some well publicised exceptions to the small scale of autobiographies by people with disability, such as *Annie's Coming Out* (Crossley and McDonald 1984), the story of Ann McDonald's institutionalisation and her ensuing legal fight to leave the facility, later made into a movie. John Roarty's *Captives of Care* (1981) described the relationships between people living in an institution, the bleakness of 'care' there and the importance of resistance to the group in fighting against the more extreme rigidity of imposed rules. This book was also later made into a movie. Heather Rose both wrote and starred in the movie *Dance Me to My Song* (de Heer and Rose 1998), which paints an intimate picture of the emotional and physical abuse inflicted on Julia by her support worker. Although the film was fictionalised and not a documentary, Heather has said in interviews that when writing the screenplay she drew from her lived experience as a woman with severe cerebral palsy.

These autobiographies together paint a picture of deprivation and ill treatment. However, that is not their sole, or perhaps even primary contribution. They are important voices of resistance, of personal growth and stories of people developing a degree of power over the structural forces that contained them while they were abused. While resilience and resistance are important themes in each of the works, they do also highlight the differences in the lives of the authors and many people with disability who remain living within disability services systems – it is no coincidence that only one of these authors is still engaged in the disability services system.

What can we learn from the experience of other marginalised groups?

The literature on abuse of other groups of people has a considerable amount to contribute to our understanding of emotional abuse and neglect of people with intellectual disability. The value of this material lies in the fact that research into the experiences of other groups, particularly children, is differently developed from the literature into abuse of people with intellectual disability. Consequently, models of understanding emotional and psychological abuse have developed and been considered in alternative ways.

Caution must be exercised in comparing the abuse experiences of people with intellectual disability with other groups of people. The life path and experiences of adults with intellectual disability who live in formal disability services is considerably different from that of children, women and elderly people. Their experience of discrimination and marginalisation is different and their historical experience of isolation and segregation is certainly different. However, there is value in drawing from these models and frameworks of understanding abuse to develop a more robust understanding of the features of emotional and psychological abuse and neglect of people with intellectual disability, particularly the focus on resilience from the women's abuse field and the shared conception of the damage that emotional abuse does to children.

Emotional and psychological abuse and neglect of children

There is considerable research addressing the emotional and psychological abuse of children, both in Australia and internationally. One of the primary benefits of this literature when applied to people with intellectual disability is its focus on the development of clear definitions and criteria for identifying emotional and psychological abuse and for the clarity with which some of this research distinguishes between emotional and psychological abuse.

There is agreement among child abuse researchers that the experience of emotional and psychological abuse is more common than usually recognised and more commonly experienced than other forms of abuse (Glaser 2002; Iwaniec et al. 2006; Tomison and Tucci 1997). This is primarily due to the categorisation of emotional and psychological abuse as generally underpinning other forms of abuse (such as sexual and physical abuse), as well as occurring without those other forms of abuse being present.

The child abuse literature contains a far stronger emphasis on the impact, outcomes and damage done to children by this form of abuse than does the literature in either the disability or elder fields. There is consensus in the literature that the impacts of emotional and psychological abuse and neglect on children can be severe, far reaching and have a myriad of consequences (Glaser 2002; Kairys, Johnson and Committee on Child Abuse and Neglect 2002), all centring on the damage done to the child's sense of self and their understanding of the ways in which they relate to the people and world around them.

A further division exists in the literature around the distinction between emotional and psychological abuse. The bulk of authors do not distinguish between emotional and psychological abuse, considering them to be the same thing. Child abuse theorists, such as Glaser (2002), state that cognition and emotion are inseparable and it is therefore unnecessary to make a distinction between emotional and psychological abuse. O'Hagan (1995, 2006) does distinguish between the two forms, arguing that emotional abuse will impact on children's socialisation and social life and impair their understanding of emotions in themselves and others. Psychological abuse will undermine the child's attempts to understand the world around them and make it familiar and manageable, confuse and frighten them and impair their confidence.

Emotional and psychological abuse and neglect of older people

A considerable volume of work has been written on the issue of elder abuse, predominantly focusing on the domestic sphere and the interaction between elders and carers (Bennett *et al.* 1997; Slater 2000). A significant amount of this literature focuses on recognition of abuse and strategies to counter it. Biggs, Phillipson and Kingston (1995) identify the need for a multilayered approach to understanding the emotional and psychological abuse and neglect of older people. They focus on the individual situation, the organisational level and also the higher systems level at which interactions and understandings of power dynamics impact on caring relationships. Futher they note the importance of taking histoircal context into account. This has clear parallels with disability researchers' analyses of the causative factors of abuse of people with disability, as discussed earlier in this chapter.

Elder abuse writers appear to find more common ground with the women's abuse and domestic violence literature, arising from a concern that elderly people and children occupy very different social, political and structural places in society. Several researchers have noted that both elder abuse and child abuse paradigms have been constructed by professionals, with the aim of protecting people and 'solving' the problem. They have not grown from a grass-roots, feminist perspective, as has the domestic violence and women's abuse literature. Abuse of people with intellectual disability clearly falls into this category, and it is valid for us to note the need for the involvement of people with lived experience of harm in defining, recognising and designing responses to abuse and neglect.

Emotional and psychological abuse and neglect of women

The literature on emotional and psychological abuse and neglect of women is almost wholly within the domestic sphere. The bulk of the literature relates to spousal abuse, or abuse within intimate relationships (e.g., Barile 2002; Champagne 1999). As with the elder abuse field, there is a considerable volume of material that focuses on the defining and understanding of emotional and psychological abuse and strategies for women, first, to extract themselves from its grip and, second, to recover from it. Here the literature differs from the other areas – the disability, child and elder abuse fields focus much more strongly on identifying potential impacts of abuse and very little on how people can recover from the experience.

Packota proposes considering emotional and psychological abuse on a continuum. On one end are isolated hurtful behaviours that may occur in any relationship; at the other end is 'pervasive, one-sided, severe psychological torture' (2000, p.4). McKinnon (2008) also subscribes to this view and draws a useful distinction between emotional and psychological abuse in the domestic violence arena. She contends that there is significant overlap between verbal abuse, emotional abuse and psychological abuse, but that they are three categories of abuse. She argues that:

Emotional abuse almost always incorporates verbal abuse and psychological abuse almost always incorporates emotional abuse. Verbal abuse becomes emotional abuse when it continues over time and has the potential to negatively affect the target person's emotional development and behaviour. Emotional abuse becomes psychological abuse when it continues over a prolonged period, incorporates a power differential and has the potential to erode the target person's sense of self and social competence. (2008, p.12)

In theory, distinctions between the forms of emotional and psychological abuse can be seen; in practice, it may not be as easy to distinguish between them. Certainly, the bulk of researchers in the field have not felt the need to dwell on the distinction. However, McKinnon's understanding of psychological abuse is very pertinent to an analysis of abuse of people with disability that draws on the use and relations of power (as is conducted in this chapter).

A distinction between emotional and psychological abuse, in which psychological abuse represents a deeper, longer term, power-conflicted set of circumstances in which a person's sense of self and social competence is threatened, may be very useful to this research. It may help to understand how long-term institutional practices help to create a 'client' and to create a set of circumstances in which the continued mistreatment of people with intellectual disability is almost inevitable.

Building from experience: a framework of emotional and psychological abuse and neglect

Drawing from the literature on abuse and neglect of people with disability, children, older people and women, a framework for understanding emotional and psychological abuse and neglect was developed for this research (Robinson and Chenoweth 2012). The framework provides detail on a possible range of abuses that could occur in this domain, and allows for the classification of those abuses into key theme areas. A tool for recognising some of the behaviours that occur in this sort of abuse and neglect has also been developed that visually represents some of the features of this form of abuse (Figure 2.1). It builds from a history of work in the abuse field, including that of Kovener (2000) and the Duluth model (Domestic Abuse Intervention Programs undated).

Figure 2.1 Emotional and psychological
abuse and neglect framework

Emotional and psychological abuse and neglect framework

At the centre of the wheel is the misuse of power and control. The key assumption of the framework is that the experience of emotional and psychological abuse and neglect in disability accommodation services is intimately connected to abuses of power and control. This assumption builds from the literature on power relations and on conceptions and constructions of disability that influence service design and delivery (Chenoweth 1995; Mandeville and Hanson 2000; Marsland *et al.* 2007). This body of work consistently holds that imbalances of power and control are inherent in disability services and, if unaddressed, create a climate in which abuse and neglect are likely to occur, as discussed earlier in this chapter.

There are occasions in the lives of people with intellectual disability where it may be appropriate, and even necessary, that others take control – for example, where someone is in the grip of a seizure or where a person is in imminent danger. However, these individual actions of control need to occur within a broader framework that addresses the balance of power and control between person and worker in order to minimise the risk of abuse and neglect.

Within this climate or systemic environment, the experience of emotional and psychological abuse is conceived as encompassing several characteristics. These characteristics, or themes, have been drawn from the child, women's, elder and disability abuse literature as earlier discussed. They are:

1. Terrorising: coercing; threatening to hurt; frightening; intimidating; withholding basic support and rights; terminating relationship and leaving the person unattended; reporting non-compliance with a programme; unnecessarily using more intrusive equipment; using consequences and punishments to gain compliant behaviour; pressuring the person to engage in fraud or other crimes.

2. Corrupting/exploiting: socialising a person into accepting ideas or behaviour that oppose legal standards; using a person for advantage or profit; training a person to serve the interests of the abuser.

3. Caregiver privilege: treating the person as if they are a child or servant; making unilateral decisions; defining narrow, limiting roles and responsibilities; providing care in a way to accentuate the person's dependence and vulnerability; giving an opinion as if it

were the person's opinion; denying the person the right to privacy; ignoring; discouraging; prohibiting the exercise of full capabilities.

4. Isolating: controlling access to external relationships (friends, family, neighbours, community); controlling access to phone, television, news; limiting employment possibilities because of caregiver schedule; discouraging contact with the case manager or advocate.

5. Minimising, justifying and blaming: denying or making light of abuse; denying physical and emotional pain; justifying rules that limit autonomy, dignity and relationships for programme's operational efficiency; excusing abuse as behaviour management; excusing abuse as caregiver stress; blaming the disability for the abuse; saying the person is not a 'good reporter' of abuse.

6. Withholding, misusing or delaying needed supports: using medication to sedate the person for agency convenience; ignoring equipment safety requirements; breaking or not fixing adaptive equipment; refusing to use or destroying communication devices; withdrawing care or equipment to immobilise the person; using equipment to torture the person.

7. Degrading: punishing or ridiculing; refusing to speak; ignoring requests; ignoring person; harassing; humiliating; ridiculing the person's culture, traditions, religion, sexuality; ridiculing personal tastes; enforcing a negative reinforcement or behaviour programme the person doesn't consent to.

8. Neglecting: failing to provide nurturance; failing to provide stimulation.

While the themes of degrading, terrorising, corrupting/exploiting and isolating are common to all abused groups and environments, the themes of caregiver privilege, minimising, justifying and blaming and withholding, misusing and delaying needed supports are used here specifically in relation to the 'care' environment.

The child abuse literature also offers categories of rejecting and denying emotional responsiveness (Tucci and Goddard 2003). In the disability accommodation services setting, these have been incorporated into the concepts of caregiver privilege and minimising, justifying and blaming. It should be noted, however, that this definition and model are specific to this environment.

Neglect is included in the wheel, but conceptually needs to be seen as an integral part of emotional and psychological abuse, where the omission of action may be as damaging as the commission of abusive action (as in the case of a person who does not learn to use a communication device due to lack of staff assistance to do so). Neglect can be seen in (at least) two ways, as a failure to provide nurturing or emotional support and as a failure to provide stimulation.

This framework for understanding emotional and psychological abuse and neglect was tested for trustworthiness against the experiences of the people with intellectual disability who participated in the research (Robinson and Chenoweth 2012). It is critical that a definition or framework has resonance with the lived experience of people with intellectual disability in order to accurately reflect the sorts of abuse that they endure. There are weighty cultural, environmental and organisational pressures brought to bear on the experience of abuse that influence both the way in which it is experienced and the way in which it is responded to. Some of these pressures influence the descriptions of abuse and may result in definitions of abuse that are dominated by a professionalised understanding of abuse, with service responses to allegations of assault uppermost in mind, rather than an understanding developed from lived experience.

Opinion on expansive definitions of abuse and neglect is divided in the literature. Some authors consider the range of abusive behaviours to be virtually inexhaustible and contend that there is risk in developing a 'checklist' of abusive behaviours, particularly in the case of abuses that may not have tangible indicators (Conway *et al.* 1996; Veith 2004). This may encourage formulaic responses – if a worker discovers that an abusive behaviour is not on the list, for example, then there is a risk they will not take action to end the abuse occurring in the life of the person with intellectual disability. As Brown maintains: 'it is the *identification* of abuse within the context of a number of more or less closed interlocking systems that is problematical rather than the definition' (1999, p.97).

Several practice and policy manuals reviewed in the course of this study contain checklists of physical indicators and behavioural signs of abuse. There is a difficult balance between providing guidance for staff who may not perceive emotional or psychological harm without some assistance and narrowing the conception of emotional and psychological harm to such an extent that service recognition to it is formulaic and only occurs to particular instances of its occurrence. The work of Page, Lane and Kempin (2002), for example, includes an analysis of the environmental and cultural causative factors of abuse and neglect that places a checklist in a broader context. Without this context, there is a considerable danger that workers may not have the knowledge and skill needed to interpret behavioural or physical indicators of abuse effectively, or to take appropriate action if they do.

There is also a body of research that builds a case that the disability sector focuses far more on responding to abuse once it has already occurred than on preventing it from occurring in the first place (Marsland *et al.* 2007; Page *et al.* 2002). In part, this may be due to a lack of capacity to recognise the more subtle signs of abuse. Women With Disabilities Australia (2007) points out that any definition needs to incorporate the structural roots of violence so that analysis can be meaningful, and Bright cautions that:

> Producing definitions, while useful to those whose work involves them in writing policies and procedures, may have the effect of disguising the routine indignity that many people may be exposed to day by day, throughout the day and possibly night time too. (1999, p.128)

However, in order to better understand a comparatively under-researched and little-considered form of maltreatment, there is value in developing a framework for understanding emotional and psychological abuse and neglect that goes into some detail in describing the sorts of behaviours and interactions that can occur when it is inflicted and is tested against the experiences of people who have experienced this sort of abuse and neglect. In a climate in which gross physical and sexual abuses of people with intellectual disability are often poorly responded to, there may be even less hope of subtle abuses being recognised and acted upon without clear and direct identification through definitions that have been developed with people who have lived through the experiences themselves.

Chapter 3

What Does This Mean for Practice?

This chapter discusses the international and domestic legal contexts within which emotional and psychological abuse and neglect are situated, before moving on to a discussion of the research on influencing factors of quality in service provision for people with intellectual disability. The relationship of service structures to abuse and neglect is canvassed and a failure identified in making connections between the features of good practice and the way most of our services are provided to people with intellectual disability. This is demonstrated through the way that several countries have responded to the results of inquiries into abuse and neglect.

Legal responses to emotional and psychological abuse and neglect

International human rights instruments, criminal law, civil law and discrimination law remain the primary legal avenues open to people with intellectual disability who experience abuse. However, the literature and legal experts are united in the opinion that legal avenues do not offer an easy way forward for people with intellectual disability to gain redress for wrongs done to them through emotional and psychological abuse. There are very significant barriers in the legal systems that are tested to the limit by people with intellectual disability and may preclude even their access to the system, much less a successful outcome.

United Nations Convention on the Rights of Persons with Disabilities (UNCRPD)

The UNCRPD (United Nations 2008) puts the experiences of people with intellectual disability into a citizenship framework, where expectations are that they will have the same rights and the same expectation that their rights will be enacted, as other members of the community, regardless of the resource limitations or other historical limitations of the disability services sector, which have previously limited the responses of inquiries into abuse of the rights of people living in accommodation services.

All of the articles in the Convention could relate to the experience of emotional and psychological abuse and neglect in some measure. The Convention recognises in the preamble: 'the universality, indivisibility, interdependence and interrelatedness of all human rights and fundamental freedoms', and the counter to these freedoms is the fundamental interrelatedness of abuses. However, some specific articles have particular relevance, including:

- Article 13 – Access to justice
- Article 14 – Liberty and security of the person
- Article 15 – Freedom from torture or cruel, inhuman or degrading treatment or punishment
- Article 16 – Freedom from exploitation, violence and abuse
- Article 17 – Protecting the integrity of the person.

However, as an international human rights instrument, 'reasonably available' domestic remedies must be exhausted before a person (or their representative) is able to take action against a government for a breach of their rights. In practice, this is a very substantial barrier to legal action in the abuse context, where the standard of proof in legal actions is such that people with intellectual disability are rarely successful in prosecuting their assailants, due to the private environment in which abuse is usually carried out and the difficulties that many people with intellectual disability may have in relating their experiences.

A recent report by the UN Special Rapporteur on torture and other cruel, inhuman or degrading treatment or punishment (Nowak 2008) expresses particular concern about this frequent experience by people with disability. The report states: 'in many cases such practices, when perpetrated against persons with disabilities, remain invisible or are being justified, and are not recognized as torture or other cruel, inhuman or degrading treatment or punishment' (p.9).

Legal redress for emotional and psychological abuse and neglect

As one legal academic points out: 'You don't want to bring in the legal system if you can avoid it. It is clumsy, slow, stressful, expensive, and you hardly ever get the outcome you expected' (Mathews 2009).

However, legal redress should be open to people with intellectual disability in the same way that it is for other people in the community who have had their rights breached.

Legal avenues do not appear to offer an easy way forward for people with intellectual disability to get redress for emotionally and psychologically abusive treatment they receive in disability accommodation services. Many of the behaviours that occur within emotional and psychological abuse are not perceived at law to be criminal, unless they occur in concert with other criminal acts such as rape, physical assault or theft, in which case they may be treated as causing nervous shock, pain and suffering and adverse impacts, although only in limited (and usually extreme) circumstances. Civil law is expensive, and is usually a case of an individual taking on an organisation and their insurer. Discrimination law is more readily accessible, but runs an attendant risk of linking abuse to policy responses rather than criminal sanctions.

Influences on quality of service provision

The literature shows a high degree of consistency around the features of effective approaches to accommodation and support for people with intellectual disability. They are fundamentally linked to a focus on the individual and to supporting and facilitating the connection of the person in a range of relationships and with a range of communities of their choosing.

MacArthur (2003) identifies some of the features of current good practice in daily living support organisations as being flexible service structures with flexible staffing, operating with flattened management structures. They separate the provision of housing and support, operate within flexible provision of housing and are not locked into bricks and mortar. Individual clients have freedom to move around the service structure according to their need and preference and they are encouraged and supported to use other personal supports and to access generic services.

Additionally, a range of researchers identify features of effective approaches as recognising and responding to:

- the importance of the relationships people have with family, friends and community and working in a way that respects and resources these relationships

- decision making and authority that is vested in people with intellectual disability and their families and supporters

- the need for the preferences and demonstrated enjoyment of people with disability to dictate their living arrangements

- the need for skilled and well-trained staff

- a strong focus on planning – not just about service activities, but about things needed to live a good life. Part of planning relates to service activities, but only as far as how they contribute to a higher goal

- choice by people with disability exercised over both day-to-day and large-scale issues

- engagement in ongoing domestic and personal activities

- the importance of ordinary patterns of living

- the need for multiple strategies to promote and facilitate the inclusion of people with disability in the community

- support of good health

- change over time – in the way people are supported, the amount of support, where support is provided and how it's provided. (Felce 2000; Finlay, Walton and Antaki 2008; Mansell *et al.* 2007; O'Brien 1993)

Empirical studies on the quality of service provision to people with intellectual disability have shown that community living models have, in many cases, not delivered on the promise of a fully included and valued life in the community (Clement and Bigby 2009). The quality of life of people living in group homes has been consistently demonstrated to be superior to that of people living in institutions, but not as high as for people living in more individualised arrangements (Emerson 2004;

Stancliffe and Keane 2000). However, studies also note that there is a high degree of variation within models of supported accommodation – to the extent that a well-run institution may provide better quality of life than a poorly run group home. As Felce notes:

> The high variation in outcomes between ostensibly similar examples of community housing services implies that there is not yet a complete understanding of the factors which are necessary within the design and operation of services for a decent quality of life to result. (2000, p.35)

This lack of definitive evidence makes it harder to differentiate between good and poor quality options for funding and government endorsement. In a climate where cost is of increasing importance to governments, the lack of hard data on the superior performance of a particular model over others means there is considerable risk that governments will make cost effectiveness their primary consideration in funding new services for people with intellectual disability.

Relationship of service structures to abuse and neglect

It is argued that there has been a fairly pragmatic and linear movement between legislation, policy and practice in disability services. This linear shift fails to give adequate space to reflect on the issues surrounding the 'big picture' of abuse and neglect, such as culture, environment and the impact of funding rules and regimes. The result of this approach is a service framework that has significantly improved in terms of its acknowledgement of the categories of abuse and neglect. However, it is questionable whether the incidence, experience and responses to abuse and neglect have been affected by these changes.

Page *et al.* found in a national review of abuse prevention strategies in Australian disability services that development of abuse prevention within state departments:

> has typically been reactive, following major service reviews or investigations that have identified systemic and extreme abuse. There does not appear to be a consistent approach to identifying, examining and learning from patterns of abuse and violence across the broad range of service types and experiences of people with a disability. (2002, p.84)

The inclusion of abuse and neglect in policy and procedure for services is essential so that staff and management may have consistent ways to respond to its occurrence. However, the policy focus does give rise to a situation where abuse and neglect may be considered to be primarily policy issues for services to address, rather than potentially criminal issues for justice agencies to respond to. The inclusion in a policy set may lead workers and managers to treat abuse and neglect as behaviour management, staff management or as programmatic problems.

Other organisational factors also impact on the experience of emotional and psychological abuse and the recognition and response to it, including social isolation of residents, due in part to ineffective planning and support from service providers and the increasing casualisation of the workforce. The increasing number of casual staff in particular has serious implications for the recognition and response to patterns of abuse and neglect, as there are a dearth of long-term moral witnesses to note the cumulative effect of this maltreatment (Clapton 2008b; Mandeville and Hanson 2000).

White et al. note this trend in their research, recognising that: 'while at a theoretical level there is a recognition of the diverse causes of abuse, popular explanations appear to give little attention to the broader context of care, instead emphasising the role of the individual' (2003, p.8).

The tendency to respond to abuse and neglect only on an individual level and to treat symptoms rather than causes of abuse is well recognised in the literature. The failure of organisations to proactively address risk, and broader systemic concerns about power and its misuse, social constructions of disability and the ambivalence of social attitudes to people with intellectual disability are all key in understanding the phenomenon of abuse and neglect (Johnson 2012; McCarthy and Thompson 1996).

The history of accommodation services has been one in which control and decision making have been vested in the staff and management who work in the services. As Brown writes:

> The life history of many of the adults with intellectual disability who live in these services is one of institutionalisation, poor medical and health treatment, poor nutrition and education, and non-existent support to redress issues of justice such as rape, assault, and theft of possessions. (1997, p.28)

This may not be a current experience for people, but it creates a particular context and history that affect their current experiences. This mode of operation has shifted to some extent, with more innovative services working to create environments in which the choices and decisions of service users are facilitated and respected. However, these choices and decisions are most often at the level of 'Jam or peanut butter' and very rarely centre on important decisions such as whom to share your home with, which staff will be employed in the service or how funding should be prioritised (Finlay *et al.* 2008; Robinson and Chenoweth 2011).

Policy responses to abuse and neglect

There is evidence of stronger policy frameworks for *responding* to abuse and neglect in Australia and comparative countries over the past five years. In Australia, policy is supplemented in several states by a working with vulnerable people criminal history check for prospective staff. In some instances staff training has increased. Since the introduction of the UK government safeguarding framework for vulnerable adults, *No Secrets* in 2000 (UK Department of Health and UK Home Office), and its Welsh and Scottish equivalents, responses to abuse and neglect in the UK have changed substantially.

Responses to concern about abuse and neglect are situated at the local level and have a multiagency focus. Adult protection boards, comprising members of relevant government agencies, are responsible for the investigation of safeguarding reports made to them that express concerns about the welfare of people at risk of harm (for example, see North Somerset Safeguarding Adults Partnership 2009). After extensive consultation in 2008, several areas were reported by a multiagency review as needing particular attention, including the need for stronger leadership in relation to safeguarding at a national level, a need for statutory powers for local safeguarding bodies and a clearer relationship between adult safeguarding, incident reporting, complaints and sustaining personal safety (Bonnerjea 2009).

However, less activity is evident regarding the *prevention* of abuse and neglect. It appears that while principles connecting prevention and inclusion are emerging in government policy in recent times, there may be inadequate attention to resourcing prevention and to making meaningful the connection between abuse and the protective factors in the lives of people with disability.

The fundamental finding of a large-scale review contracted by senior government policy administrators in Australia (Page *et al.* 2002) concerned the need for primary prevention of abuse through the development of inclusive communities, advocacy, building individual resilience and family supports and intervention. Australia is currently developing a policy of national individualised funding and support, due to commence in trial sites in 2013. Attention to safeguards and abuse prevention in the developmental work surrounding this framework is present, but limited.

UK government policy includes explicit recognition of the tension between protection and empowerment and includes principles that articulate prevention and protection as part of a broader social care agenda that also builds on personalisation, plurality and partnership (Department of Health 2010). The discussion of Winterbourne View in the following section, however, provides a commentary on the difficulty of translating principles into practice when a fundamental requirement of an appropriate environment in which to live remains unmet.

Fyson and Kitson identify a failure of disability policy makers to make the necessary connections between what they term two: 'parallel agendas' (2007, p.429) – the desire to promote choice and independence for people with intellectual disability on one hand and on the other the need to protect them from abuse and neglect. They argue that this failure can be seen in two ways. It may result in increased risk to more independent people through ignoring the reality of the risk in their lives that comes with having control vested in others who provide support. Conversely, people may be overly controlled through risk management approaches that ineffectively acknowledge their right to self-determination in an effort to keep them safe.

An underpinning feature of services funded by governments across a number of countries is a focus on compliance to a predetermined set of guidelines and regulations. Compliance mechanisms such as these rely heavily on audit and regulation to monitor specific elements that have been identified as markers of quality in service provision. Clegg, in her work on holding services to account, points out that audit is a very different process from evaluation and one that does not aim to search for knowledge about the operations and drivers of service. She writes: 'Audit investigates adherence to government policy' (2008, p.581). This is necessary to create a benchmark level of service quality, but is a missed opportunity for opening debate about how to improve supports and the effectiveness of supports and does not focus on the measurement of individual outcomes for people who use the service, aspirations of either individuals or organisations or, in this case, the protection of people from abuse.

One of the perhaps unintended results of applying a managerial approach to human services is a service structure that prioritises the management of systems over the meeting of individual need (DiRita, Parmenter and Stancliffe 2008). It gives rise to a culture in which compliance with statutory standards and monitoring of administrative tasks and functions are of primary importance (Goggin and Newell 2005), and one in which the act of management is more important that the subject of management – as seen in the 'content free' management that has so frustrated human services practitioners over the past decade (Wills and Chenoweth 2007).

In the case of preventing, recognising and responding to emotional and psychological abuse and neglect of people using services, a compliance-based approach is unlikely to uncover the more subtle abuses that appear in people's everyday lives, due to its concentration on the measurement of the existence of policy and procedure and the extent to which procedure adheres to policy. This comes at the expense of measuring more relevant indicators of success in preventing and responding to this harm, such as the perceptions of people using services; their experiences of harm; and the degree to which services have been able to scaffold supports around people that act as preventative measures against emotional harm.

Inquiries into abuse and neglect

Inquiries into situations where allegations of extreme abuses have been made in several countries, mostly in large-scale institutional services. In Australia there have been several judicial inquiries into abuse of people with intellectual disability living in accommodation services since 2000. Two of these inquiries concern the same institution, the Basil Stafford Centre in Queensland. The first inquiry, the Stewart Inquiry found that the abuses were so pervasive that there was little alternative but to recommend the closure of the institution at the earliest opportunity. Among the findings were that:

> An insidious culture existed at the Centre. This culture promoted the occurrence of client abuse and gross neglect, and the harassment or intimidation of staff members who reported or could have reported

such occurrences, by other staff members. This culture provided the climate, and thus the opportunity, for acts of official misconduct to take place and minimised the likelihood of both the act and the offender being detected. The situation existing at the Centre had the effect of discouraging, to the point of stifling, the reporting of such acts of official misconduct. The situation cannot be explained away as arising from the actions of a few individual 'bad apples'. (Stewart 1995, p.xii)

Prior to the release of this report, the Director General of the relevant department informed the judicial commission that the Centre would be closed within three to four years. Despite this clear central finding and this public undertaking on the part of government, four years later, the Centre was still operating and a second inquiry was held into allegations of abuse in the same facility. The Carter Inquiry (Carter 2000) discusses the reduction in the number of residents living in the Centre (from 111 to 69) and the intention of management to further reduce this over time to approximately 25 people. Despite identifying poor management and negative staff attitudes as significant problems, the inquiry concludes that the Centre is a viable concern and should remain open in a reduced capacity. It promotes vigilance in the community-based Adult Living Service, the group home-based service to which many people had moved, giving caution about the risk of the culture of abuse moving into this system.

At the time of writing, it is proposed that new villas will be built on the grounds of the old Centre to contain people who require secure housing due to challenging behaviour. It seems that the risks of abuse and neglect for people due to isolation and institutionalisation are not abating with time and knowledge of alternatives.

Benbow (2008) notes this trend in the UK, identifying the failure of British human services systems to learn from inquiries. The Winterbourne View Hospital abuse investigation and subsequent criminal conviction of 11 workers for assault and horrific abuses against residents with intellectual disability also highlights the interrelationship between individual and systemic harm. While these workers have been convicted of crimes and civil offences against the people they harmed and the investigation has resulted in the closure of the facility, a number of residents who have moved to other care facilities have since been the subject of further safeguarding orders – it seems their experience of harm has not ended by moving from this particular place (Mumford 2012).

Serious case reviews are an important part of the UK safeguarding framework, aiming to identify opportunities to improve practice and process across all agencies involved in the care of adults at risk. This serious case review identifies major systemic issues, ranging from significant concerns in the original commissioning of the facility with a private for-profit provider that paid insufficient attention to safety and resident wellbeing through to communication failures on the part of agencies, which resulted in a whistleblower not being responded to. Underpinning the recommendations of the review is a clear recognition of the fundamentally inappropriate nature of the facility and the need to develop more effective supportive alternatives for people with high and complex support needs (Flynn 2012).

In the USA, inquiry reports on abuses of residents in institutional environments in Texas (Chung Becker 2008a), New York (Biben and Bearden 2011) and Nebraska (Chung Becker 2008b) indicate that these concerns are transcontinental. Of significant concern is the fact that a long list of abuses and systemic issues were identified for resolution in both Texan and Nebraskan facilities *prior* to extreme assaults that later became the subject of criminal charges. This connects closely to the work of Wardhaugh and Wilding (1993) on the corruption of care and to White *et al.* (2003) and Marsland *et al.* (2007) all of whom identify systemic power relations and means of engagement which preclude or make difficult the resolution of abuse and neglect, as discussed earlier in the chapter.

A managerial, procedurally driven, approach to responding to the abuse and neglect of people with intellectual disability seems to influence the policy response of services supporting people with intellectual disability. At a broad level, there appears to be little responsiveness to the recommendations of commissions of inquiry into abuse in residential facilities. Legislation, policies and procedures are predominantly focused on responding to individual instances of abuse. While it is, of course, essential that individual cases of assault, injury or abuse are dealt with effectively and with compassion, there is little evidence that legislation and policy is also focused on changing environments and interpersonal dynamics that may allow abusive cultures to develop and be sustained.

PART 2

Stories of Lived Experience

Sally: And so, while that was going on, were you telling people the things that were happening, when he [another resident] grabbed you?

Jim: Yes! They didn't want to know.

Sally: They didn't want to know.

Jim: Cause they all go to one side.

Sally: Beg your pardon?

Jim: On one side.

Sally: They all went on one side? On the other fellow's side?

Jim: No, the service.

Sally: The service's side? Oh.

Chapter 4

Insult and Injury

In this chapter, the narratives of people with intellectual disability and family members are presented. It begins with a discussion of the method used to conduct the research. A summary of the volume and range of the abuse people experienced is provided, followed by the narratives of people with intellectual disability and families about this harm. Their experiences are ordered according to the categories of emotional and psychological abuse and neglect identified in the framework outlined in Chapter 2.

Approach to the research

While this book does not aim to be a research methodology text, before entering into the stories of the nine narrators, it is helpful to briefly visit the research approach that was used to develop the narratives with each person and how their material was respected and used in the research. It is important to address some of the difficult ethical dimensions of research that arise in working with people on sensitive and difficult issues, to share what worked well for other researchers and in practice and also to share what didn't go so well.

In doing this research, an attempt was made to resolve some of the barriers precluding the involvement of people with intellectual disability in research about their experiences of harm. This was through crafting a narrative-rich approach, narrative collage, which privileged the participation of people with intellectual disability, drew in supporters who could bolster their narratives and facilitated the control over the narratives by the key narrators with intellectual disability – and which could include the counterstory of resilience that may be part of their abuse stories.

Narrative methods in disability research have been gaining currency over the past decade. Popular in research with other marginalised groups, particularly women, children and older people (see for example, Montalbano-Phelps 2004; Nandlal and Wood 1997), narrative approaches are increasingly used with people with disability (Owens 2007; Tregaskis and Goodley 2005). There is, however, limited reach into narrative research with people with significant support needs due to their cognitive impairment. Much of the narrative research with people with intellectual disability to date has been with people who can provide informed consent, who can construct linear narratives and who have good recall of events.

A number of writers, particularly from the UK, have considered the principles and practicalities of involving people with intellectual or learning disabilities in research as partners, as advisors and as participants (Atkinson 2004; Chappell 2000; McClimens 2008), and this book draws directly from this material.

In order to help people tell their stories of abuse, a methodology that included people who have a range of capacities was needed, which minimised the risk of distress to them and drew on people's strengths. The sensitive nature of the research topic made this need even more pressing. Finding an ethically workable methodology that could keep the focus on people with intellectual disability, while valuing and including the participation of those who supported them and who had valuable contributions to make, was challenging. There was a need to respect the primacy of people's narratives, but also to acknowledge that there are limits to people's memory, knowledge of service responses to abusive and neglectful incidents or policy and practice contexts that may cast a broader light (Booth and Booth 1996).

Narrative and agency

A number of researchers highlight problems in ascribing agency to people with intellectual disability who may not understand the processes with which they are engaged. A different approach for people with what Kittay (2001) refers to as 'attenuated agency' was crafted for this study, drawing on the knowledge of family members and advocates close to people with high support needs.

Those people who have not directly taken part in the study are nonetheless critical to its conduct. While their experiences are included through proxy accounts – the narratives of their family members and advocates – they were personally unaware of the research. No claims could be made to individual involvement of people with high support needs, although the experience of participating in the research may have been beneficial (or not) for family members in similar ways as for people with intellectual disability.

Ethical issues

Significant ethical issues arise in considering research that includes interviewing victims of abuse about their experience. These are compounded for people with intellectual disability, due to their potential difficulties in having insight into the possible personal repercussions of involvement in such research.

The capacity of people with intellectual disability to consent to participating in research of this nature is a clear issue of ethical concern. Clegg (2004) and Clapton (2003, 2008a) both discuss a hermeneutic approach to ethics as critical to the production of research in this context – putting particular emphasis on the creation of an ethical environment. This ensures that the individual consent of participants is not the only mechanism to ensure the fairness of the research process. While the research was conducted within the framework of university ethics guidelines, it also builds from a body of theoretical and applied research about maximising the participation of people with intellectual disability in research by putting the onus on the researcher to make the research space easy to understand, fair and ethical.

Narrative collage

Narrative collage was crafted as a methodology that might enable people with intellectual disability to have a privileged position in the research, but draw in and welcome the valuable input and support of others close to them.

The primary goal in using narrative collage was to develop something that was greater than the sum of its parts. Each constituent part tells a story, but the sum of the parts together make something that is new and conveys a theme or meaning that none of the component parts suggests so well alone. Narrative collage is fundamentally about gathering collective experience to develop new understanding. Kostera (2006, p.14) frames it in the following way: 'The point with composing a collage out of the collected stories is to find a collective level in the invention.'

Underpinning the collection of narratives are some key principles that sit alongside traditional narrative research practice. First, that control of the development of the narrative collage is vested in the person with intellectual disability where possible – the number of meetings, content and flow of discussion and decisions about who else to approach to offer a contribution to the collage. Second, that the final collage is 'signed off' by the person with intellectual disability or that they are in full knowledge of what is in their collage. In the case of this study, these were transcripts of verbal interviews but there is no reason that they might not be posters, photo essays or video logs. Third, people are offered the opportunity to see how their collage sits against other people's experiences by having (dis-identified) access to preliminary results of the research.

Using the method

A total of nine narrative collages were constructed for this study. Of these, four were narrative collages created by people with intellectual disability and allies in their lives – family members, advocates and service providers. Five collages were developed without involvement of people with intellectual disability, due to the high support needs of those people. Their narratives were created by proxy – by family members and advocates who knew them well.

The project was overseen by two advisory groups – one comprised advocates and the other was made up of people with intellectual disability who were experienced in research. Each group gave specialist advice and assistance on the relevance and appropriateness of the proposed approach, the content of the interviews and on recruitment strategies. It proved very helpful to have two concurrent groups, as their focus proved quite different. For example, our advisors with intellectual disability told us it was particularly important that people were in control of who participated in the making of the collages and a key focus area for our advocate advisors was on strategies to minimise risk to participants.

Recruitment of participants was conducted using purposive sampling. Due to the significant potential of the research to cause distress, gatekeepers were used to reach people with intellectual disability. Disability advocacy organisations were asked to identify people they thought would meet the criteria of being interested in the research; able to consent to participation; unlikely to be distressed by participation in narrative interviews; not living where the abuse happened; and not in a therapeutic relationship about their abuse or neglect. Once identified, we asked those advocacy providers to give an easy English information flyer to prospective participants and to ask permission for us to make phone contact with them if they were interested in being involved.

The use of gatekeepers to participation was a vexed issue. While not wishing to be unduly protectionist, we were also aware of the risk of distress that was possible in speaking at length about long-term abuse and neglect and felt it important that people were not left isolated at the end of the research process. No-cost access to a counsellor skilled in working with people with intellectual disability was available as part of participating in the research, but the need for ongoing supportive relationships was apparent.

A series of interviews were conducted with each participant with intellectual disability. The original intent was to commence with an introductory meeting, at which the researcher and participant could meet, the study could be explained in detail and the consent process worked through. This meeting was to be followed by a set series of three semi-structured interviews during which the narratives would be constructed with people. This built from Seidman's (1998) three-phase interview structure, in which the first interview sets the scene, the second interview allows participants to reconstruct details of the experience and the final interview encourages them to reflect on the meaning of the experience.

In practice, people had been waiting, sometimes for years, to speak to someone about their experiences and it was hard for them to get through the consent process without talking about their abuse, much less pace their experiences over a three-stage interview process. A far more organic interview series developed, where people met several times with the researcher, until they felt their story had been told. This ranged between one and five meetings. Family members, advocates and support workers who bolstered the narratives generally met on one occasion, either face to face or by phone, according to preference and distance.

A further meeting, sometimes two, was offered to participants to review their transcripts (on tape, CD or written format) and the narrative collages. While people were keen to have their words, and to have them in formats easily accessible to them, none of them wanted to go over their transcript, or their collage, with the researcher. Similarly, when summaries of the results of the research were provided, no participants took up the offer to meet and discuss them, although people were interested in the outcomes of the study.

In addition to narrative collage, more traditional, semi-structured interviews were conducted individually and in small groups with 16 policy makers, service providers and advocates.

Analysis

A fundamental dilemma also arose in the research design, in trying to determine how to make sense of both the range and nature of abuses and neglect experienced by a group of people (and what this may mean for other people living in disability services), while still remaining alive to the meaning and worth in the individual stories of each person who was involved in the research.

The narratives were taken apart and analysed thematically in the research, in order to try to understand what makes up this sort of abuse and neglect. It became apparent that the story of each person's 'service' life was important in both its detail and totality. The separateness of the incidents is important, because in and of themselves they are important as individual wrongs. However, the cumulative effect of them is another level of wrong that was done to people and needs to be seen to be so.

Narrative collage proved a useful methodology for privileging the participation of people with intellectual disability in research on a difficult topic. It was a structured and helpful way to draw in supporters and, at the same time, to hold the person with intellectual disability in the centre frame and manage the participation of others so that it did not overtake that of the person who found it most difficult to participate in the narrative process.

This method enabled people with intellectual disability to focus on the parts of their narrative that they felt comfortable telling and that they remembered. In a number of instances, developing a narrative flow helped people with recall and they related either complete events, or partial events that could be followed up with supporting participants for further details. Linked to this was the fact that people did not have to get bogged down in trying to remember dates, bureaucratic details or the order of the places in which they had lived (some people had lived in upwards of a dozen accommodation services), as these details could be followed up later with the supporters nominated by the person.

Clearly, there are limitations that must be acknowledged. This is a small-scale study, in which the method was used only with people who could give consent to participate. Narrative collage with people with intellectual disability is also a dense method, requiring considerable time in rapport building and development of trust with participants and also gatekeepers, transcription and development of alternative format information and in checking the veracity of the narrative collages with key participants. All of this activity occurs prior to holistic and thematic analysis, already considerable investments in time, energy and skill.

Ongoing tensions between the voices of people with intellectual disability and the voices of other participants in research need to be acknowledged and continual efforts made to balance them. In this research project, there were three data sets – the narrative collages; narratives of family members of people with intellectual disability with very high support needs; and interviews with systemic advocates, policy makers and service providers. While narrative collage was an effective way to privilege the voice of people with intellectual disability, in the broader study, it still remained a challenge to ensure their voices were not subsumed by more policy friendly, quotable or sophisticated words.

Narrative collage is an attempt to overcome the limitations of time passed, history, power, inarticulateness and ability to generalise that combine to impact on the capacity of people with intellectual disability to talk about their experiences, particularly experiences that are negative. The approach seeks to understand how individuals are impacted by their experiences. It is also a methodological effort to understand the impact of people's experiences in a more systemic way, by analysing the narrative collages alongside other narrative and qualitative data that may uncover some of the shared features of their experiences that highlight key concerns and opportunities. With further testing, it may be a useful addition to the suite of tools we can use with people with intellectual disability so they are engaged and in control of their participation in research about their lives.

Overview of the experiences

A brief consideration of the volume of abuse that people have faced may assist in situating their narratives in a broader context. While this is a narrative study, including this quantitative representation opens an alternative view of the nature of the abuse experienced that may not be seen through the narratives alone.

The table presents a cumulative total of the number and range of emotional and psychological abuses that were related by people with intellectual disability and their family members and supporters. The abuse they described is spread over the time in which they have used services, which for all participants except Diwata was at least ten years. In the case of five of the nine participants, they had lived in disability services from the time they were young children.

Table 4.1 Volume of emotional and psychological abuse and neglect related by participants (ordered by frequency of experience among participants)

Type of abuse	Number of references to the abuse in the interview data	Number of participants experiencing this form of abuse
Caregiver privilege	53	9
Terrorising	36	7
Minimising, justifying and blaming	35	9
Degrading	34	9
Isolating	29	9
Neglecting	25	8
Withholding, misusing or delaying needed supports	11	5
Corrupting/ exploiting	5	3
Total	**228**	

It is also worth noting that some things were just too hard for people to talk about. There were several incidents that family members decided, on reviewing the transcripts, that they would prefer to keep private, as they were too painful to include. There were also some experiences that participants perhaps weren't ready to talk about – a number of people had 'false starts' in conversation, where they did not complete thoughts or sentences about abuse experiences and were obviously uncomfortable. There is little doubt that there was more abuse and neglect in people's lives than is presented here.

The remainder of the chapter is devoted to the narratives of participants concerning their abuse and neglect experiences. They are discussed within the categories of emotional and psychological abuse and are ordered according to the frequency with which they were experienced by people with intellectual disability. At the end of each section there is a summary table highlighting the key features of the abuse and neglect experiences. The first of these is caregiver privilege.

1 Caregiver privilege

Caregiver privilege includes:
- treating the person as if they are a child or servant
- making unilateral decisions
- defining narrow, limiting roles and responsibilities
- providing care in a way to accentuate the person's dependence and vulnerability
- giving an opinion as if it were the person's opinion
- denying the person the right to privacy
- ignoring
- discouraging
- prohibiting the exercise of full capabilities.

All people involved in this study experienced emotional and psychological abuse that falls into the category of caregiver privilege. It was the most commonly reported category of abuse related in the interviews, with 53 separate episodes of abuse noted across the nine participants.

Caregiver privilege at the individual level

Some of the experiences people described were about how individual staff members exercised caregiver privilege over them, or about the abusive relationship they had with a particular staff member.

BEING FORCED INTO THE PASSIVE 'CLIENT' ROLE

Tom talked about how his current support worker ruined his Christmas dinner. He had bought a piece of pork to roast for his Christmas meal. He asked his support worker for help to cook it. He told the story:

Tom: She said, 'I haven't got three hours or however long pork takes to cook'— it takes a few hours. She said 'I haven't got time to sit here and watch it cook! I'll take it home and I'll bring it back.'

Sally: She'll bring it back cooked?

Tom: And when I asked her about it, she said, 'Oh, I had to throw it out to the dogs because it was slimy.'

Sally: But you'd only just bought it, had you?

Tom: She cooked it and left it sitting out.

Tom ended up going to a church group for Christmas lunch. The worker was not disciplined, despite Tom complaining to the service coordinator, and Tom was not recompensed for the meat. Tom has asked the same worker not to remove paperwork from his house. She has taken it home, regardless, to complete it. She has also taken Tom's house key from the key safe to get more keys cut, despite him not wanting workers to have keys to his home.

Caregiver privilege at the systemic level

Much more common in the narratives were people's stories of abusive experiences that were caused by staff following service policies and routine practices that did not adequately respect their rights. These practices, procedures and policies seemed to focus much less on the needs of individuals and much more on the convenience of the system. There are several key areas in which caregiver privilege was experienced by people who were involved in this study – in how personalised their care was, the level of control and decision making they were able to exercise, the relationships with support workers they had and in the action taken when they complained about unfair treatment.

BEING A COG IN THE WHEEL

The way that clothing and services were provided en masse to several people in the research was depersonalising, limiting and sometimes degrading. While it no doubt made it easier for the facilities to function, it had the effect of increasing people's dependence, limiting their capacity and painting them to staff, families and other residents as not worthy of the respect of personalised service.

Craig remembered the way that clothing and services were provided when he was growing up, living in an institution for children with disability. Staff used to pick clothing off a shelf in a clothing room for children, and dentists, doctors and physiotherapists all came in to the institution instead of children being taken to visit them outside of the institution.

Patrick remembered buying his brother Dan a new shirt and bringing him home for a weekend to discover that a staff member had written his name on the shirt on the outside of it in permanent marker. When Patrick raised this, no-one at the rehab hospital was 'interested in changing that or anything'.

Rose felt so strongly about the poor quality of care in the service that her daughter Jenny was living in as teenager that she felt she could not go away on a holiday. Jenny used a respite service, which was bad for similar reasons. Rose said: 'it was just like a churn out. Nobody took any care of the washing, it was just all thrown in together, nobody had anything personal, everybody sat down, they didn't give a stuff what you were eating. It was revolting.'

FIGHTING FOR CONTROL

Having control over the decisions, large and small, that make up a lifestyle was expressed by almost everyone in the research to be important to them. Being treated as a child and having decisions made for you was a particularly strong concern for Tom and Jim. Getting information from staff about health, accommodation changes and major incidents in the lives of people with high support needs like Jill, Rose, Dan and Fran was a major problem for their families.

Tom remembers living in a group home where he had no say in whom he lived with. When someone died, another resident was moved in without any consultation with other residents. Tom felt this was unfair. In his current living arrangement, he is able to decide who will support him, although in observing his relationship with his support workers over our three meetings, his stated control and his actual control of the relationships are very different and the support workers do not display a great deal of respect for him.

As an adult, in his current service, Jim feels as if he gets the chance to make little choices but not big ones. For example, he recently did not want to employ a support worker he met, as he thought she looked as if she was a drug addict. However, he felt he didn't have any option but to say yes, due to pressure by the service to take her on. His mum, Wendy, also talks about phoning Jim and that often he will be having a 'snack' dinner, like spaghetti on toast. She feels that he often eats what is convenient for staff, rather than what is healthy for him.

At several points when Fran was a child, the institution proposed that there would be major changes in her care, with minimal notice and no consultation. For example, one change proposed was that only one staff member would be rostered between two cottages at night to support ten residents who have high support needs, including someone who had uncontrolled epilepsy. After strong protest, this was overturned – however, it was part of a pattern of action where changes that were not in Fran's best interests were initiated a number of times without consultation or prior agreement.

NARROW CONCEPTIONS OF PERSONHOOD
Rose was concerned that Jenny might be depressed. She expressed this concern to Jenny's current support workers, saying that she was worried that Jenny may be low because she's not going anywhere exciting. Their response to her was that her life was better than many other people with intellectual disability, so there is no cause to worry.

INCREASING DEPENDENCE
Some people talked about experiences of care in which they, or their family member, became more dependent as a result of the actions of the service, rather than better supported to live their life.

Patrick used to spend time with Dan at the rehab hospital, trying to stimulate him. He felt that the staff resented him 'revving' Dan up, and would have preferred him not to be stimulated. Patrick says:

> you know, one of the nurses said 'Oh, it's alright for you, you come out here and spend a couple of hours' – it was more like six hours – 'and then go away and leave him and we have to deal with the [sic].'

Because I would take him out walking along the fence and all sorts of other stuff to try and stimulate him. And you know, 'You're doing this and we've got to deal with the consequences.' And I said 'Well, that's what you actually get paid for.'

At one point, Jenny was living in a service in which people had individualised supports, singly or in groups of two. A new manager could not see the rationale behind this and changed the orientation of the service, so it became a standard group home model. Fortunately, Jenny had portability of funding, but the disruption of what was a workable arrangement had a significant cost.

BREAKING THE RULES

Several people recalled receiving inappropriate or even offensive responses when they protested about treatment that they felt was unfair – responses that emphasised the power of the organisation over the people who lived in it.

Jim remembered being put to bed at seven o'clock through his teen years by staff, despite not being tired. After he complained, he was put to bed later, although he says staff 'weren't nice about it', and there was obviously a cost to making the complaint. Patrick also recalls Dan being put to bed at six o'clock in the evening and staff expressing their dissatisfaction about the fact that he used to yell out through the night – due, Patrick feels, to the fact that he had had enough sleep by about midnight.

When Diwata moved to a regional town several hours from her family, the service took rental properties that were on short leases. Every three months she and the other children were required to move into new premises. This happened three times in succession. Every time her dad, Datu, visited her or took her home for a short time, on her return Diwata would get very upset. Datu decided to bring Diwata home, and was taken to court by the service over what they said were unpaid fees – strongly disputed by Datu. The result of this court action was that Diwata's financial affairs are now managed by the Public Trustee, and Datu has to account for all her spending. Datu felt that: 'Just like, I'm losing the right for my daughter.'

Caregiver privilege at the structural level

At the broadest level, caregiver privilege can be seen in the way that programmes of supported accommodation are implemented in Australia, particularly in the lack of choice and self-determination afforded to people with disability in their accommodation and support arrangements.

Ivy felt that conditions for people with intellectual disability hadn't improved very much with the programme of devolution of institutions. She said:

> From what I see of it, people have been moved into mini institutions all over the community now. They're in three-person and four-person households all round the community, and living in more or less the same conditions they lived in [institution]. So I really don't think they've done good service to the exercise. I think that they caused a lot of upset to a lot of people for no good reason.

This table summarises the key features of the abuse of caregiver privilege experienced by participants, dividing the themes that emerged from the results into individual, systemic and structural domains.

Table 4.2 Summary of caregiver privilege

Individual	Systemic	Structural
• Staff acting to protect their own interests • Being forced into the passive 'client' role to meet worker convenience	• Being a cog in the wheel • Fighting for control over decisions • Narrow conceptions of personhood • Care provided in a way that increased dependence • Being punished for 'breaking the rules'	• Accommodation and support system is unresponsive to personal choice and self-determination • Accommodation and support system defaults to institutional practices, whether institution or group home

2 Terrorising

Terrorising includes:

- coercing
- threatening to hurt
- frightening
- intimidating
- withholding basic support and rights
- terminating relationship and leaving the person unattended
- reporting non-compliance with a programme
- using more intrusive equipment
- using consequences and punishments to gain compliant behaviour
- pressuring the person to engage in fraud or other crimes.

Eight of the nine people with intellectual disability in the study had experienced terrorising. Ann, Jim and Tom talked about multiple experiences of being terrorised, in their narratives, and all five family participants shared their knowledge of experiences their family members had been through. In total, 36 separate experiences of being terrorised were related. Several themes emerged within these experiences, including the use of punishment to gain compliance, being intimidated and being threatened. Almost all abuse within this category is themed within the systemic level, with few experiences categorised at either the individual or structural levels.

Terrorising at the individual level

INTIMIDATION AND CONTROL

Rose described a pattern of behaviour by a staff member who supported Jenny, which she was concerned about. Jenny broke her wrist when she fell out of bed. They went to the hospital and the support worker met them there. When the hospital staff did not follow the protocol for treating Jenny that Rose had recently completed with the specialist disability clinic (attached to the hospital), both Jenny and Rose became agitated. When Jenny began hitting and kicking, Rose began to use the strategy she had worked out with the clinic previously to calm Jenny and contain the situation. The support worker told Jenny to 'stop it', and she did. This is not Jenny's usual pattern and she has a long history of complex challenging behaviour. Rose was very concerned that Jenny stopped out of fear of the support worker.

Later that day Rose drove Jenny to her house. Jenny couldn't get out of the car without help and Rose asked the support worker to wait while she went around to the other side of the car, so she could push from one side, while the support worker steadied Jenny from the front. Rose said the support worker instead: 'yanked Jenny out, literally yanked her!' That night, the support worker did not give Jenny the prescribed dose of pain relief medication for her broken arm, saying later to Rose that it was not necessary, even though Jenny is not able to say whether she is in pain.

Rose later found out that the staff member reported Rose to the manager of the service, saying she was disruptive and rude to the hospital staff. She has also complained to the service manager about Rose before, saying that her involvement in Jenny's life is stressful for workers. Rose felt that she had no option to respond. She has seen this support worker treat Jenny roughly, but has no evidence of assault or physical abuse. She said: 'I've got no way of proving that, and if I even said it, that would be harassment.'

Terrorising at the systemic level
INTIMIDATION

Being intimidated was almost a 'feature' experience of this form of abuse and it underpins many of the other elements of the category.

Ivy recalled things getting very bad at the institution where Jill lived towards the end of her time there. The government had put in place a devolution programme, and was encouraging parents to move their adult children from the institution into group homes. This was challenging for some parents, particularly those people who had been strongly encouraged to place their sons or daughters in the institution years before, on the grounds that it was a safe and permanent solution for them. Ivy was engaged in a robust fight with the government for adequate funding for Jill to live with only one co-resident, not in a group environment. She also remembered an alarming conversation with another mother. Ivy said:

things got so bad at the centre, and I would say deliberately so, because they wanted us to want our people out. One mother told me she was told that in time to come, there would only be very violent men living at [institution], and she had a daughter. So that was some encouragement to move your daughter out of there!

When Ann lived in the psychiatric institution for a year, she recalled the time-out room with anxiety. She said several times: 'You only had to look out the window to go into time out!' She remembered it as being extremely cold and the worst part about being in the institution – a place to be scared of.

Jim remembered being locked up, when he lived in the institution. He doesn't know why he was locked up, and thinks it was something that probably happened to everyone.

LIVING IN A STATE OF FEAR

Some experiences were so constant that they amounted to a continual state of fear at some points in people's lives.

Ann described an environment at the hostel where physical violence from staff to residents, and between residents, was frequent. She related several incidents of physical assault, including being hit by other residents, being hit by staff, being prevented from leaving the premises by other residents acting on the instructions of staff and being threatened with physical violence by staff. She said: 'I was frightened there every day. That's why I used to take off and go and see Andrew.' Andrew, Ann's mental health case manager, used to return Ann to the hostel and leave her there, after notifying the owners of her complaints.

Gemma (Ann's support worker) said that the legal action against the owners of the hostel that Ann took, with a lot of encouragement and support from her advocate and sister, brings her both a measure of relief and a great deal of anxiety. Ann was also one of subjects of a prominent television documentary programme about the quality of care in the facility, which aimed to expose some of the abusive practices. She showed me this programme, and was at the same time proud and nervous about her participation.

Amanda recalled an incident that eloquently described the longstanding emotional and psychological impact of abuse. She remembered the day when she realised that it was likely that Fran had been physically assaulted in the past and that the assault had left its mark on her emotionally. Fran had left the institution and was living in her own home. Amanda and Fran's support workers used to try to encourage Fran to work out her frustration by punching into their hands. Amanda said:

> And one day, I remember, I held my hands up, and I must have looked threatening, and the look on her face! She was absolutely terrified. And so that said to me, I can't prove anything, but that says to me that she was physically abused.

BEING THREATENED

Physical and emotional threat was experienced by several participants in the research. This is closely linked to intimidating and frightening.

Jim had personal possessions stolen on numerous occasions, by both workers and co-residents. A worker stole Jim's collection of two-dollar coins from his bedroom. One co-resident who stole from Jim threatened him when Jim complained about the theft. He threatened to tell the police about Jim complaining about him. Jim was very frightened by this man and very relieved when he eventually moved to another house. The service took little action to redress the problem, Jim recalled.

Ann also related the experience of being threatened by a worker at the hostel, when she had been physically assaulted earlier that day. She had decided at lunchtime that she'd had enough, and she was going to 'take off' and go home to her family home. Another resident knocked her over to prevent her leaving, bruising her. She went back to her room and lay down. Her sister called, and the weekend supervisor let her take the call as a favour (usually, Ann was expected to walk down to the public phone box in the street). Ann remembered the supervisor standing over her and saying 'Don't you dare say anything' before handing over the phone and then staying in the room for the length of the phone call. She said did not feel able to tell her sister what had happened but that she felt her sister knew something was not right: 'from my voice'.

THREATS ESCALATING TO ASSAULT

Sometimes threats escalated to actual assault, leaving people injured and vulnerable in several ways.

One particular incident that Ann recalled involved being pushed down the stairs at a boarding house she lived in previous to the hostel in which most of the abuse she discussed occurred. Ann had been on the phone to her mother and the phone had cut out. She asked the staff member for more money for the pay phone but was told to wait, as the staff member was giving out medicine. Ann objected to waiting, and in the resulting argument, the staff member pushed her down the stairs. Ann was physically injured in the fall and it appears she was also evicted from the hostel for fighting, as she left immediately for another hostel, not of her choosing.

On another occasion at the hostel, Peter, the owner, came into Ann's bedroom and accused her of tipping coffee over a table. Ann said he dragged her to the top of the stairs and held her over the stairwell, threatening to throw her down the stairs. Ann said: 'He said, "You'd better watch your step, or I'll be ringing your sister"… He was so strong, he could really hurt you.'

COERCION

In some cases, it was not clear to people whether their rights had been abused or not.

A support worker took Jim's best shoes to give to her boyfriend. Wendy considers this theft, but Jim wasn't sure. The worker seems to have talked Jim into giving her the shoes, as Jim didn't wear them often because he rarely goes anywhere that he needs to dress up. Wendy complained, and the worker gave back the shoes, but Wendy said they were 'well and truly worn' by then. The worker was not disciplined, to Wendy's knowledge, beyond being spoken to by the manager.

USING PUNISHMENT TO GAIN COMPLIANCE

The use of physical and emotional punishments to gain compliance incites fear in the person receiving the punishment and aims to ensure that they will not use the behaviour in future. However, in some of the following instances, the link between the person's behaviour and the punishment are tenuous at best.

When Jim was young, he remembered a particular night nurse hitting him every time his stoma bag came off and making him put it back on himself. At another facility, he was put to bed without dinner if he came home from school and his stoma bag had come loose. Jim said that at one stage this was happening every second day.

Ann's co-residents also used to share the same sorts of experiences. Ann related the story of a roommate who had epilepsy, who was punished for having seizures. She said:

And if she had been good and hadn't had a fit all week, she could go away for the weekend to her boyfriend's. I had to hold her tongue to make sure she wouldn't get in trouble for having a fit. If I had've let it go and she had that fit, no weekend leave.

Datu said that every time he visited Diwata at the group home where she was living, she was upset. Whenever he took her home for a break, she would cry all the way back (a three-hour trip):

Datu: She doesn't stop. She just feels sad and things.

Sally: Oh.

Datu: And I've got no choice, 'cause it's for her, it's good for her, to learn things. She learned, but not too good.

Sally: Why do you think she was feeling sad?

Datu: She hate the place. [firmly]

Sally: Do you know why?

Datu: Oh, probably 'cause some people who look after her, you know, they're not treating her so good, something like that. I don't know, but so far, that's what I know. She's not very happy, and every time she says one of the ladies, like, give her a smack, things like that. I don't know.

WITHHOLDING BASIC SUPPORT AND RIGHTS

Basic support and rights were withheld from people in a number of different ways, resulting in them going without fundamental requirements for periods of time and going through a great deal of stress.

Tom was receiving a certain amount of hours of support each week from a non-government service provider. He attended a review meeting, at which he heard them say they would continue their service. He said he then received a letter saying: 'Bye bye mate, you've got to leave,' as he was too hard to manage. He was not referred to a new service provider, and he and his mother had to go back to the government funder to renegotiate his hours of support as a matter of urgency. For a period of several months Tom was in a difficult position, with inadequate support hours and having to use casual and agency staff.

After Ann was released from hospital once her broken hip was stabilised, the owner of the hostel moved her to a group home she owned in another suburb. Here, Ann remembered being bedridden and lying in her own urine. She recalled being given a poor diet of only fruit, in order to make her lose weight and said that the staff who worked there were not nice people, who spoke roughly to her most of the time. After a period living here, Ann was admitted to another hospital with bedsores and sores on her feet.

The table below presents summary information about the key features of terrorising as a form of emotional and psychological abuse and neglect, as expressed by participants.

Table 4.3 Summary of terrorising

Individual	Systemic	Structural
• Intimidation and control by an individual staff member (acting outside of a policy framework)	• Intimidation • Living in a state of fear • Being threatened • Threats escalating to assault • Coercion • Using punishment to gain compliance • Withholding basic support and rights	

3 Minimising, justifying and blaming

Minimising, justifying and blaming includes:

- denying or making light of abuse
- denying physical and emotional pain
- justifying rules that limit autonomy, dignity and relationships for a programme's operational efficiency
- excusing abuse as behaviour management
- excusing abuse as caregiver stress
- blaming the disability for the abuse
- saying the person is not a 'good reporter' of abuse.

All nine people involved in the study had experienced this form of abuse and neglect, and 35 separate incidents were related in the narratives. Themes that emerged in this category centred on denial, justification or excuse. The first of these concerned a failure to acknowledge abuse, assault or injury by staff and services, or making light of it by not reporting it to family members and also denying the physical and emotional pain of injury and abuses that people had experienced. The second theme of justification involved the imposition or following of rules that limit autonomy, dignity and relationships for the sake of the efficiency of the operation of the service. Finally, the third theme to emerge here was around excusing abuse as behaviour management.

At the broadest level, there are a further two themes that have relevance to the study – concerning cultural abuse and the 'boxing' of people with intellectual disability into categories that they do not fit, in order to meet programmatic or funding guidelines.

Minimising, justifying and blaming at the individual level

It is difficult to separate the individual from the systemic with regard to people being treated as 'poor reporters' of abuse. While Ann's experience is a clear example of abuse on the part of an individual worker, it can also be viewed as a signal of an under-resourced community housing and support sector.

Ann used to find the constant fighting between residents at the hostel where she lived distressing and upsetting. She used to leave and go and see Andrew, her mental health case worker, seeking another alternative to living at the hostel. In her interview, Ann remembered the following experience.

Sally: Did you talk to Andrew about it [specific abuse problem Ann had raised]?

Ann: Yeah, but he just rang them and, he just got the wrong side of the story. He just used to put me in the car and take me back.

Sally: Right. And so after he called them, he didn't think that you were telling the truth?

Ann: Mmm. Manipulative.

Sally: Is that what he said?

Ann: Mmm.

Ann was treated as a 'poor reporter' of abuse, and her case worker's approach to her reports of ill treatment was to alert the abusers to her complaints and then return her, unsupported, to the environment in which the problems had occurred. Ann's abuses were eventually substantiated by her advocate and sister and some of them were the grounds of legal action against the owners of the facility.

Minimising, justifying and blaming at the systemic level

As with other categories of emotional and psychological abuse, systemically rooted action is behind most of the incidents that people shared in their narratives. These included the failure to acknowledge injury or assault, blaming the person's disability for the abuse, denying their pain, excusing abuse as behaviour management, and enforcing rules that limit dignity for the sake of efficiency.

Not acknowledging, or making light of, injury or assault

The lack of proper acknowledgement of injuries and possible assaults on people with high support needs, who were unable to say what had happened to them, was of great concern to their family members.

Amanda recalled several times in Fran's younger years when she was concerned about physical injuries Fran sustained, which were not adequately explained. She described a climate of frequent concern by she and her husband for Fran's wellbeing, where injuries were not reported to them and where they had no proof of what she called their 'niggles' that things weren't right.

Over the years, Fran had two lots of stitches. Amanda said she does fall frequently, and bangs into things often, so the injuries may well have been accidental, but the causes were not detailed by the institution staff. Once, Fran came to school from the institution with a bruise on her cheek about the size of a tennis ball. In Fran's communication book between school and the institution, the institution staff had written only that there was bruising. The institution did not contact Fran's family to let them know she had been injured and did not contact the school to explain the injury. Fran said: 'Now, it could have been done by another resident. The bruise on the cheek, how did that happen? You just don't know. And they could have acknowledged that it happened, don't try and say that it didn't happen!'

Amanda took Fran to her own doctor and Fran's dad photographed the injuries. After a complaint to the state Ombudsman, the institution apologised for the way they had handled this incident, but Amanda felt that little change occurred as a result of the complaint.

Jill was left at the regional country fair when the workers returned to the institution with other residents, leaving her sitting on a wall in the showground. Jill is unable to stand on her own and remained sitting on the wall until ambulance officers, who were fortunately located in a nearby tent, became concerned about the length of time she had been sitting there alone. When she was returned to the institution by the police, at around seven o'clock that night, she still had not been noticed missing by staff. After she was returned to her unit on the grounds of the institution, staff phoned the institution doctor, wanting to check that Jill hadn't been sexually assaulted or physically harmed. Ivy said:

And the doctor said that she was finishing her shift in 20 minutes, and she didn't have time to come down and examine her, and that they'd have to wait until the next doctor. When the next doctor came on, he said he'd have to do his rounds, and he wouldn't be finished until 9 o'clock, and by that time she'd be asleep. And they wouldn't come down and make sure that she was alright.

Ivy was not notified of any of this, but discovered it all ten years later, on obtaining Jill's file through Freedom of Information legislation when Jill moved out of the institution.

When Jim shared a house with another resident who had challenging behaviour, staff and coordinators routinely told him that the other man had more problems than he did and that Jim needed to be understanding. When the other man threatened Jim, banged the door near Jim's head and shouted at him, Jim rang the supervisor for help, as there were no staff at the house with them in the evenings. He was told that he would have to ignore him and that the other man couldn't help it. Jim said the service did not do anything that helped him to feel safe while he was living with this person. When Jim complained about another co-resident having loud sex with a blow up sex doll in his bedroom while Jim's sisters were visiting, he was told that there was nothing they could do – it was the private business of the man, and Jim would just have to put up with it.

When Jenny and Rose were in a medical environment, a nurse broke confidentiality and told them that four non-verbal residents from the institution where Jenny was living had been brought in to the sexual assault unit over the past month. Rose was horrified and got together with another parent, and they went to the director of disability services for the state at that time. He acknowledged that the assaults were occurring and told Rose and the other mother that they knew the assailant, had removed him and would be putting him back on duty in the institution when things had 'died down'. Rose said she was then told that she could buy a new wardrobe for Jenny, something she had been asking to do for some time.

BLAMING THE PERSON'S DISABILITY FOR THE ABUSE

Despite the fact that people who participated in this study lived in specialist disability accommodation services, it was sometimes their disability that was blamed for the abuse that occurred in their lives. This was the case for both Jill's chemical abuse and Dan's challenging behaviour.

Ivy feels that Jill was placed on epilepsy medication after having one large seizure as a reaction to a combination of three other drugs, and may not have epilepsy. Two of these drugs were strong psychotropics. The other drug was to control dribbling, about which Ivy says: 'The dribbling doesn't bother Jill, it only bothered the workers, because they had to keep changing her apron, you know.'

When Jill left the institution, Ivy, in consultation with Jill's doctor, weaned her off all medication except for a small dose of the epilepsy medication, with no ill effect. She is now in good health and takes half the dose of Epilim she was taking in the institution and no other medication – Ivy questions whether any of the other drugs were needed by Jill at all.

When Dan first moved into the rehab facility, his brother, Patrick, felt that he wouldn't have thought of himself as a 'patient', and that he would have found the place 'pretty creepy'. Dan had an incident early on in his stay there and the manager asked his family to come and take him home, due to his behaviour. Patrick refused, and the facility sent Dan to the psychiatric ward at the local hospital, which assessed him and returned him to the institution. Patrick says their diagnosis was: 'he doesn't have a psychiatric problem, he has behavioural problems. This is what you do'. The service promoted itself as a centre of excellence for people with complex needs, but refused to accept responsibility for supporting Dan with challenging behaviour.

DENYING PHYSICAL AND EMOTIONAL PAIN

The denial of both physical and emotional pain by services and workers can be both physically abusive and also emotionally and psychologically abusive.

Jim remembered being taken on an outing in a bus one day with a group and getting his foot badly burnt on the exhaust pipe of the bus. Jim requires support to move onto and off a bus, as he uses a wheelchair and has no use of his legs. The service took Jim straight to hospital for treatment, but Jim said that: 'I got in big trouble for it,' when his foot was burnt, despite the fact that he had no control over where his feet were placed and, in fact, could not feel the burn occurring.

To Ivy's sorrow, she only discovered through reading Jill's file after she had left the institution that when Jill first entered the facility, she was in a state of severe emotional distress. Ivy recalled:

> I kept phoning and I was getting 'Oh no, she's doing well', but when you read the file you see how upset she was, that's why she was on all the Melleril and all the rest of it, because she was so distressed.

EXCUSING ABUSE AS BEHAVIOUR MANAGEMENT

The use of behaviour management strategies that people did not adequately understand the rationale behind was an experience shared by several participants. Jim, Craig and Ann all shared the view that being locked up or hit were experiences that are standard, happened to most people and that they were not sure why they happened to them. This form of behaviour management is an obvious physical abuse and also has clear emotional and psychological consequences.

Jim remembered being locked up several times when he lived in an institution as a child. Once, he was locked in a playground with some other residents after he had complained about something. He felt that this was a punishment for complaining. Another time, he was locked in a cupboard, but he doesn't know why this happened. On a third occasion, Jim remembered being locked in a room for a long time, although he doesn't remember having done anything wrong. He thought they probably did it to everyone who lived there, but wasn't sure – it was a long time ago.

When Jim was a teenager, he lived in a hostel that housed ten teenagers with disability. He used to be put to bed at seven o'clock, which he complained about as being too early. After he complained, Jim said:

Jim: They make it hard.

Sally: How did they make it hard?

Jim: They didn't talk to me nice and treat me nice.

After he made the complaint, Jim was put to bed later, but staff completed the task in such a way that it was an unpleasant experience for Jim.

Datu also recalled Diwata telling him that she was 'smacked' by a worker at the house where she lived, he thinks when they: 'couldn't agree or something'.

ENFORCING RULES THAT LIMIT AUTONOMY, DIGNITY AND RELATIONSHIPS FOR THE SAKE OF SERVICE EFFICIENCY

Some of the service policies that are intended to provide choice and to increase the level of self-determination of people with intellectual disability are operationalised in such a way that the opposite occurs. For example, over the weeks that Jim was meeting with me to tell his story, he was also interviewing prospective support workers. He said that he did not feel able to say no, if he didn't like the person. He did tell the coordinator of the service that he did not want one particular person to work with him, but the coordinator overruled him, saying that it was so hard to find support workers, he would have to give her a try. Wendy, Jim's mother, also raised this, saying that Jim doesn't really get to choose his own staff, although he is supposed to.

Jim's firm belief that he is not allowed to have a cordial relationship with support workers (see 'Isolating', p.100) is a disheartening example of the justification of rules that limit relationships for the sake of the operational efficiency of the service programme. Jim is also punished for the development of a relationship that may possibly have grown beyond a usual support worker/client relationship, either because it was not handled skilfully by the support worker or because it was a genuine friendship between two like-minded people.

Patrick recalls numerous occasions when he was told: 'that's the way it is, that's the rules,' in response to questions about why his brother could not have a particular therapy, be put to bed later, have more stimulation in his day or similar issues. His response was to say: 'And I always say, "Well, I don't give a shit about the rules, this is a human being you're talking about here."'

Minimising, justifying and blaming at the structural level

At the broader level, Patrick talked about how difficult he had found it to deal with bureaucracies and get staff to envisage Dan as a person. He said:

> I talk about the box syndrome...You know, I talk about them having boxes, and saying, 'Well, you've got to get in that box.' 'Oh, I'm sorry, my arms and legs are hanging out.' 'That's ok, we'll cut them off and put them in the box, but you've got to get in the box.'

In terms of cultural abuse, Craig's experience is a prime example of emotional and psychological abuse in which relationships, autonomy and dignity have been severely limited for the sake of the efficiency of the operation of a programme. In keeping with government policy of the time, Aboriginal people were required to obtain permission from the government to travel – including Craig and his family. He could not visit family without his grandmother's home and family members being inspected for cleanliness by a government matron prior to his visiting and him being shaved in case of lice infestation on his return to the institution. Craig's relationship with his own culture, as well as with his family, is damaged as a result of these experiences, which contain a mixture of protection and abuse.

The following summary describes the primary themes of the abuse experience of minimising, justifying and blaming that emerged from people's narratives.

Table 4.4 Summary of minimising, justifying and blaming

Individual	Systemic	Structural
• Being treated as a 'poor reporter' of abuse	• Not acknowledging, or making light of, injury or assault • Blaming the person's disability for the abuse • Denying physical and emotional pain • Excusing abuse as behaviour management	• The 'box syndrome' • Enforcing rules that limit autonomy, dignity and relationships for the sake of service efficiency • Enforcing rules that limit autonomy, dignity and relationships for the sake of programme efficiency

4 Degrading

Degrading includes:

- punishing or ridiculing
- refusing to speak
- ignoring requests
- ignoring the person
- harassing
- humiliating
- ridiculing the person's culture, traditions, religion
- ridiculing personal tastes
- enforcing a negative reinforcement or behaviour programme the person doesn't consent to.

Degrading was a frequently reported form of emotional and psychological abuse and neglect. All nine participants shared memories of degrading experiences, and 34 individual incidents of degrading abuse and neglect were described during the interviews.

Degrading at the individual level

Here, examples of degrading that were not linked to organisational or structural causes were primarily instances of punishment, where staff had taken it upon themselves to impose harsh punishments for perceived infractions, or dehumanisation.

Both Diwata and Jim were physically punished as children. Diwata was smacked by a staff member; her dad thinks because they couldn't agree on something. Jim was put to bed without dinner in one facility and smacked by another staff member when his stoma bag came off during the day. While the smacking constitutes physical abuse, Jim's strongest recollection is the humiliation.

Ann recalled the treatment she received from the owner of the hostel when she fell and broke her hip:

Sally: When you had the accident, you got taken to the hospital, you told me.

Ann: Frank piggybacked me. They were all laughing about it in the dining room.

Ann found the owner of the hostel in which she had one of her accidents, particularly embarrassing and shaming. She described many occasions when she was degraded by this woman, who routinely shouted at residents, 'grounded' them if they committed any minor transgression, refused to allow them to take phone calls and restricted access to family members. Ann felt that the injury caused by her accident was compounded by the indignity of the way in which she was treated by the owners of the hostel and other residents.

Degrading at the systemic level

As with caregiver privilege, it was far more common that experiences of degrading shared by participants in the research had their roots in the systems driving organisations and services. Where the results in degrading may differ from caregiver privilege is that at least four people identified the diffuse and pervasive nature of degradation as deeply affecting them in the long term.

THE SNOWBALL EFFECT

Amanda, in talking about her daughter Fran's cumulative experiences in disability services, said:

There's so many different types of abuse, and it all comes down to the same thing. It's making people nothing. And Fran was nothing. There was never anything nice said about her, everything was negative. And she had to put up with that, and we had to put up with that, until we all sort of believed it, almost.

Gemma, Ann's current support worker, in talking about Ann's long history of abusive experiences in boarding houses, hostels, psychiatric institutions and nursing homes, said:

the thing that was like the base ground, what I thought was degrading and neglecting was the huge assumption that you could just do that on a day-to-day basis. That was the basis of these people's life... [these things] are just really pervasive, you know?

This understanding of degradation as a daily experience at some points in the lives of people with intellectual disability was also put forward by Rose and Patrick.

PUNITIVE SERVICE CULTURES AND PRACTICES

Punishment as a practice of services was a clear theme and one that Jim in particular talked about a lot. Jim recalls being punished at the institution where he lived, by being locked up. He was locked in a room for a long time, he thinks. He doesn't remember doing anything wrong and thinks that this was what they did to everybody, but isn't sure.

Another time, at the same place, Jim was put out into the playground with other residents as a punishment and the gate closed so they couldn't get back in. He said he was put there because staff: 'didn't want to listen to me or things like that,' when he made a complaint about something.

ROUTINE PROCEDURES THAT THOUGHTLESSLY HUMILIATE PEOPLE

Some of the practices that people with intellectual disability and their family members found humiliating and undignified may not have been done with the intention of making them feel this way. For instance, the fact that Fran's bowel movements were recorded on the wall, in full view of anyone coming into the ward, was no doubt conceived as a measure to aid the management of her health. When Tom lived in a boarding house in the inner city, he had a room on the first floor. The boarding house did not have wheelchair access, and he could only get in or out of the building if other residents carried him.

THE DEGRADING IMPACT OF POOR PHYSICAL CARE

The quality of physical care provided to people who also have physical support needs has a clear link to this category of abuse. The lack of physical care provided to Ann in the hostel was also degrading. She described one night where she was unable to get to bed herself, due to her physical disability. Other residents dragged her down the corridor and laid her on the floor next to her bed, where she stayed all night.

Ridiculing and belittling

The most frequent descriptions of degrading were comments, actions and practices that belittled and ridiculed people living in disability services. Some of these were almost 'throw away' comments, although the impact of them has stayed with people and their family members, in some cases for many years.

For instance, Patrick described a meeting he had with the management of Dan's rehab unit about his care. He recalled: 'I said, "why is it that Dan gets no therapy?" And she gave me a very condescending laugh, "Oh, well it wouldn't be worthwhile, would it?"'

DEGRADING OF LIFESTYLE

One of most diffuse ways in which degrading was represented in the narratives was in the way that people's lifestyles were affected by the imposition of service structures.

Rose, for example, struggled to reconcile the difference in Jenny's lifestyle after she began living in a large disability service with how their family lived before she moved. She said:

> Jenny's life was herded into a bus to go to school, herded there to go home, and you stayed there all the time. It was terrible! This was a girl who was used to getting on a plane and thinking, 'Oooh, it's school holidays. Why don't we all go to Singapore?' or 'Why don't we drive to Ayers Rock?' This is a girl who had been around the world twice and there she was in this dump. And it was awful, and her life was ratshit. And I knew that, but I couldn't take her home, because I couldn't manage her.

Degrading at the structural level

The impact of government policy at the broadest level can be exemplified in this study particularly strongly in the degradation of one person's culture. The intersection of disability policy and indigenous policy of the day resulted in an alienating and shaming childhood and adolescence for Craig – one in which his sense of self was eroded on several fronts.

Cultural degradation

Craig's experience as a child was one in which he was degraded on both personal and structural levels for his indigenous status. As a young child growing up in an institution, Craig did not know he was Aboriginal and was confused by taunts and insults by other children that he was 'black' and 'different'. He recalled:

And I said to them, 'how can I be different' Ah, because I said to them, you know, 'I'm just the same as you, in a wheelchair, so what's the difference?', you know, and they just said 'you're black'. You know, that got me thinking.

Craig talked to the principal of his school, who told him he was Aboriginal. To be told this way was painful and affecting. Craig said: 'No-one told me about it. Not even a member of the Aboriginal race told me that I was Aboriginal. I was told that I was Aboriginal by a non-Aboriginal person.'

As an adult, Craig obtained his files through Freedom of Information and gained access to a thick folder of both useful and painful information about his past. He is referred to as 'an inmate' in parts of his file. His birth family is referred to in ways that portray them as less than human. It is also clear that he came to the institution as a baby from a situation of high risk.

Craig did return home to his birth family periodically for visits throughout his childhood, which required both permission and inspection of his family's home from government authorities, due to their Aboriginality. Craig's grandmother, with whom he stayed, was required to submit to an inspection of her home, and of the other grandchildren, for nits and scabies prior to Craig coming to visit. Looking into the files, the language used in an official letter of permission to travel gives an indication of the cultural degrading that has affected Craig deeply:

Replying to your letter dated 29th, you are advised that settlement matron and welfare officer inspected Agnes Z's home today. They report that it was clean, as was the yard. They also examined the heads of Agnes Z's children and report that they were clean.

Craig remembered coming back to the institution from these visits and routinely having his head shaved in front of the other children, which he used to find humiliating.

Reflecting on his past, Craig said: 'When I go through all this stuff, it's about emotional issues… Everything they're saying is emotionally, is emotionally abusive.'

He felt that the actions of the system, rather than individuals, have had a big impact on his life, and this impact is felt mainly through the fact that Craig feels uncomfortable with Aboriginal people. He said:

Because, even though I don't show it, I hide it, I still don't feel comfortable with Aboriginal people, because I haven't grown up with them. You know, even though I'm an Aboriginal myself, I just don't feel comfortable.

The following table summarises key features of degrading abuse and neglect that were related by participants in the research.

Table 4.5 Summary of degrading

Individual	Systemic	Structural
• Punishment for perceived infractions of rules • Humiliation	• The snowball effect of degradation of time • Punitive service cultures and practices • Routine procedures which thoughtlessly humiliate people • The degrading impact of poor physical care • Practices and policies of responding to complaints and abuse which ridicule and belittle • Service structures which degrade lifestyle	• Cultural degradation • Loss of identity

5 Isolating

Isolating includes:

- controlling access to external relationships (friends, family, neighbours, community)
- controlling access to phone, television, news
- limiting employment possibilities because of caregiver schedule
- discouraging contact with external supporters such as case managers or advocates.

As with caregiver privilege and degrading, isolating was a form of abuse that all nine participants in the research had experienced. In total, 29 separate experiences of this form of abuse and neglect were contained in their narratives.

Isolating at the individual level

The narratives of isolation that appeared at the individual level involved particular staff who took action to prevent people from having access to family, friends or community, or who in one case took malicious action to isolate people by damaging the relationships that they had with others.

For a time, Jenny shared a home with another young man. Jenny's mother Rose remembered them as being very attached to one another, but over time this relationship eroded, Rose feels, due to the intentional action of some male staff members in the house who wanted to move Jenny on. These staff made anti-female comments and, Rose thinks, incited Jenny's co-resident to develop an anti-female perspective that impacted most heavily on Jenny and also on female staff. Ultimately, Jenny was subject to physical violence from her housemate and to two years of the emotional and psychological effects of being denigrated with anti-female comments such as 'bloody women' from both male staff and her housemate.

Isolating at the systemic level

Stories of abuse at the systemic level primarily concerned service practices and policies that had the effect of isolating people with intellectual disability. In some cases, people were physically isolated; in others, socially and emotionally isolated. Service policies and practices that damaged relationships between people living in disability services and their families, which left people isolated, were described. A strong theme emerged concerning policies and practices that isolated people by excluding their families and other supporters.

PHYSICAL ISOLATION

Physical isolation was described in a range of ways. Ann, for instance, refers to being locked in the hostel in which she once lived, so no-one could get out. When Tom was living in a particular hostel, he was housed on the first floor with no wheelchair access to get in or out of the building. The only way he could get in or out was if someone else would carry him, and his wheelchair, up or down the stairs.

Medication and the misuse of disability equipment physically isolated Dan. With Dan's move into a wheelchair came an increasing control of his movements by staff within the facility in which he lived. His brother, Patrick, recalls that at the same time as Dan moved into the wheelchair, he also stopped going to a singing group he was part of. He also remembers being told of Dan's wheelchair being removed when he was in bed so he could not leave the room. Patrick had had previous arguments with staff over their dissatisfaction with Dan's active nature and their wish that he would be more compliant and less active, and he suspects that Dan's medication was increased at least partially to limit his movement.

SOCIAL AND EMOTIONAL ISOLATION

Relationships with support workers were discussed by everyone who participated in the research. Discussion of elements of these relationships is spread throughout this chapter, because the impact of these relationships, both positive and negative, is enormous. However, in terms of isolation, relationships with support workers were most commonly expressed in terms of controls over interactions and relationships between people and workers, as Jim's story poignantly illustrates.

Jim firmly expressed his view that he is not allowed to be friendly with carers who support him in his home, and he felt bitter about his experience of being penalised for feeling friendly towards workers:

Jim: You can't do that.

Sally: You can't do what?

Jim: Be, be friendly with carers.

Sally: Be friendly with them?

Jim: A couple of carers I did. One carer I got in trouble with, took me to see a psychologist.

Sally: A psychologist? So, the carer took you to a psychologist?

Jim: No, arranged for me.

Sally: Arranged for you to go to a psychologist?

Jim: Yeah. I was being friendly with her.

Sally: So, they said because you were being friendly with her, you had to go to the psychologist?

Jim: Yeah.

The organisation responsible for providing support to Jim had deemed his attachment to a support worker to be inappropriate, and organised the visit to the psychologist. Jim lives alone, does not work and has little social activity in his week. Support workers are sometimes the only people he sees in his week. His views expressed above regarding support workers leave him profoundly isolated.

Amanda said that the whole experience of living in an institution was isolating for her daughter, because: 'no-one knew Fran'. The combination of high staff turnover, low staff-to-resident ratios, an institutional environment and Fran's high support needs resulted in a living environment in which Amanda felt Fran was not well known by anyone where she lived.

Ann also talked about feeling very isolated and lonely when she lived in a hostel. She frequently used to pack her bags and leave to go somewhere else. Ann said: 'I couldn't make any friends there, cause they were too busy fighting and squabbling with each other.'

SERVICE POLICIES THAT DAMAGE RELATIONSHIPS AND
ISOLATE PEOPLE WITH INTELLECTUAL DISABILITY

The imposition of rules and regulations was felt by some family participants to actively damage the relationship between them and their sibling, son or daughter.

At one point, Patrick brought Dan home for an extended period. He had made an agreement with the main nurse manager for the district that Dan's bed costs would be covered while he was at home. Patrick received a bill for Dan's bed costs for the entire period he'd been at home, and when he contacted the service, assuming there had been an error, was told that the agreement he'd made was with an individual who had gone on leave, there was no agreement and the bill was to be paid. Patrick recalled:

> I said 'Well, OK, that's fine, he'll be back tomorrow.' And from then on, I probably went once a week, sometimes even once a fortnight, for 18 months. And I had a meeting with them, and we had reviews, which were a laugh. At one of the reviews I sat there and told their physios and nurse managers and whatever you have there, 'You know, I find it really sad that I can't come to visit someone I love because I can't deal with the institution where he lives.'

Rose remembered how difficult it was for her to go and have dinner with Jenny at the hostel in which she was living as a teenager. She recalls being the only parent who came to have dinner, and that staff: 'didn't quite know what to do with me'. She described staff at this place telling her, and other parents, about successes they'd had with residents, but in a way that seemed as if they were able to do something parents had failed to do with their children – something Rose strongly felt induced feelings of guilt and inadequacy in parents.

POLICIES AND PRACTICES OF EXCLUDING FAMILIES, WHICH ISOLATE PEOPLE WITH INTELLECTUAL DISABILITY

All family participants related experiences where they had been excluded from involvement in the lives of their family members. They felt, without exception, that this was unacceptable, in many cases abusive, and that it contributed to the patchwork of negative experiences they themselves had had, as well as those experienced by their family member.

Rose talked about the shared experiences of other mothers she knows through a support group and how service policy impacts on the degree to which they feel able to advocate for their child when they are being ill treated. Rose said:

> You want to advocate for your child cause he's going to hospital, with his head split open every six weeks, but the service says 'No, you can't, the other mothers don't want anyone going to the house without an appointment'. So no mothers go to the house.

Datu said that he could see that his daughter Diwata was very unhappy living in the service she was in, about three hours away from her family. He decided that he was going to bring her home. The service convinced him to leave her there for one more year to stay at school. Datu now regrets this decision, because Diwata was so distressed by living there and so isolated from her family.

Ivy, Jill's mother, became very involved in managing Jill's health when she had a serious health problem that was not addressed by the institution in which she lived, despite repeated attempts by Ivy to get them to take action. She took Jill to see specialists outside the institution medical structure to resolve her problem and remembers that, as a consequence:

> I was very unpopular. I'm still a bit unpopular...no, they didn't like that at all. They used to come up with all sorts of reasons why they hadn't done things, or things had happened, and it was always my fault, you know. It was always the way I'd spoken to the staff or the way I'd spoken to the manager.

Wendy, Jim's mother, recollected a brief period that Jim spent at what is now a notorious institution as a young child. While he was only there for a fortnight, the first time she went to see him, she was so shocked at his physical condition and surroundings that she brought him home again. However, it wasn't easy to visit Jim. Wendy remembers: 'You had to go through a pretty strict procedure to get into the place, too.'

ISOLATING AT THE STRUCTURAL LEVEL

At the broadest level, people with intellectual disability experience isolation as emotional and psychological abuse when it pervades their lives, characterising large parts of their existence, moving well beyond the disability service's regime. Jim and Craig have both experienced this sort of abuse.

Ivy's view that the move from institutions into group home accommodation has not necessarily afforded people with intellectual disability a less isolated lifestyle – rather, that they live a similar lifestyle in smaller groupings (expressed earlier in this chapter) can perhaps be seen in Jim's routine.

Jim said that he doesn't talk to his neighbours and he doesn't see his friends very often. He used to work, but his workplace closed down, and his health needs were increasing to the point where he was finding work difficult. His mum comes and stays a couple of times a year, for a few weeks at a time. Jim is of the view that he is not allowed to be friendly with support workers (see p.101), although they are the main people he sees in the week.

Craig's experience of isolation as a form of emotional and psychological abuse and neglect is a cultural one. Craig was removed from his family as a baby and taken to the city for medical treatment. He was subsequently placed in an institution for children with disability. He experienced profound isolation from his family, his culture and his cultural traditions, not even finding out that he was Aboriginal until he was well into his teenage years.

The summary below provides a snapshot of the identified features of isolating as a form of emotional and psychological abuse and neglect.

Table 4.6 Summary of isolating

Individual	Systemic	Structural
• Preventing access to family and friends • Maliciously damaging relationship with housemate and friend	• Physical isolation to increase staff convenience • Control over relationships and lack of meaningful relationships resulting in social and emotional isolation • Service policies that damage relationships and isolate people with intellectual disability • Policies and practices of excluding families, which isolate people with intellectual disability • Delegitimising of family relationships	• Social and physical isolation from community • Cultural isolation

6 Neglecting

Neglecting includes:

- failing to provide nurturance
- failing to provide stimulation.

It is difficult to isolate emotional and psychological neglect from abuse experiences, as many abusive experiences contain a neglectful component. It is a category that is pervasive, insidious and difficult to pin down. However, the thematic analysis identified that eight of the nine people with intellectual disability in this study experienced emotional and psychological neglect that was distinct from other abuse, in addition to neglect that accompanied other abuse. There were 25 separate incidents of emotional and psychological neglect, across a number of themes. These included the failure to maintain a nurturing environment; failure to maintain a stimulating environment; the impact of under-resourcing; the connection between physical and emotional neglect; and compounding neglect.

Neglecting at the systemic level
UNDER-RESOURCING
The chronic under-resourcing of disability services, particularly the large residential institutions of the past, cannot help but contribute directly to the emotional and psychological neglect of people who live in them. Low staffing ratios, high levels of client need and high staff turnover combine to create an impersonal living environment in which it is unlikely that nurturing relationships and stimulating programmes will thrive.

At one point, management at the institution in which Fran lived proposed to cut staffing on the night shift, to the point where one staff member would staff two villas housing ten residents, all of whom were under 18 years old. All of the residents had high support needs and one had uncontrolled epilepsy, which required a high level of monitoring. After vigorous opposition from families, this change did not occur. Amanda said:

> Can you imagine if I went out at night, and left my kids on their own? Community Services would be down on me like a ton of

bricks!…But that was the sort of thing that happened, that made you feel like they didn't really care about our kids.

Amanda talked about the difficulties that staff were faced with in the environment of the institution, which contributed directly to the quality of care that was available to Fran and others living there. One staff member was allocated to look after six people, all of whom had high and complex support needs. Amanda said: 'So you had one person looking after six, so they could never be any more than minded. So you had six children heading in different directions – how can they have anything but neglect?'

Amanda gave some concrete examples of this neglect. One time, a worker told another parent she was responsible for the care of 12 children on her own between the end of school and dinner time, all of whom required assistance with personal care, feeding and behaviour. Fran received stitches a couple of times, due to injuries received when she fell because there weren't enough staff around to care for her. She fell in the bathroom when someone was having a bath and the floor was wet, but she was in the bathroom because there was only one staff member, and in order to bathe the other person and also supervise Fran, both of them needed to be in the bathroom. This has implications both for the privacy of the person being bathed and for Fran's dignity. These are situations where individual staff members seemed to be making the best of a bad situation, but were unable to overcome the limitations of inadequate resources.

Amanda recalled the whole experience of living in the institution as being very isolating for Fran as: 'no-one knew Fran'. It is difficult to see how this failure to have anyone who really knows your preferences, your sense of humour or your tastes in food makes it possible to nurture a person.

Ivy also remembered the understaffing as a contributory factor in the emotional neglect of Jill. As with Fran, Jill lived with a ratio of one staff member to six residents. Ivy recalled:

no matter how much the parents suggested that more staff should be available, that was completely ignored. Actually one of the ministers said that if they increase staff, they found that staff pay more attention to each other than they do to the residents. So, that was the attitude to the staffing of the villas.

FAILURE TO MAINTAIN A NURTURING ENVIRONMENT

In order to sustain emotional and psychological health and wellbeing, a nurturing home environment is important for all people, but perhaps even more so for people with significant support needs due to their intellectual disability. In several cases, however, this was not the case for people who participated in the research. The failure to provide a nurturing environment is emotionally and psychologically abusive – giving people no 'safe harbour' to build their emotional reserves.

After Jill left the institution and moved into her own home, she was supported by a non-government service. The service received extra funding for one month, in the transition period, and as soon as this period was over, they started to say that there was not enough funding to support Jill and her co-tenant. Ivy felt that workers were not experienced or well trained in supporting people with high support needs such as Jill's, and staff turnover was high. Ivy gave the example of one worker who was recruited who couldn't bear the sight of faeces and who used to vomit every time she had to assist the two ladies with their personal care. The service pulled out of their contract to provide support within a matter of weeks and took the co-tenant with them to another house, leaving Jill stranded.

Ivy and Jill's advocate attended a series of meetings with senior managers at the state disability department to try and resolve the situation, during the course of which Ivy was given a sheet of paper with instructions about how she must conduct herself when dealing with service providers. The service provider was not penalised, despite a series of episodes of apparent mismanagement, including failure to adequately staff and manage the house within the budget they tendered for, allowing Jill to almost swallow a large piece of kitchen sponge and poor management of her health. While this is not directly emotional and psychological neglect, the result of this situation was that Ivy was highly stressed, and Jill was subject to a series of casual workers for the next few months until the situation was resolved – resulting in Jill living in an unstable environment, which she found stressful and distressing, and where she was not nurtured in the way that she requires in order to maintain her fragile health and wellbeing.

Craig found out as an adult that his mother had never signed release papers, which prevented him from being adopted and meant that he remained living in the institution until he turned 18. He remembered meeting a family who wanted to adopt him when he was around five years old and another family a little later who were interested in him.

This was an enormous loss to him. Craig recalled his living arrangements growing up. He slept in a dormitory with anywhere up to 20 others. Personal belongings were kept in a pigeonhole and, when he was a little older, a metal locker with a drawer. Craig had no photos or other items to make things personal.

Tom was at great pains to make sure that I was aware that he did the hiring and firing of staff in his current living arrangement. His support worker on the day that we met for one interview was a young man who had arrived an hour early for work and was waiting at Tom's until it was time to start his shift. Over the course of two hours he slept on the sofa, played music through his headphones, went outside to smoke and sprawled on a chair, answering Tom's repeated questions of: 'We're friends, aren't we?' in monosyllables, with his eyes closed. The previous week, this man's grandmother, also a support worker, had arrived to start work while I was with Tom. She entered the house without knocking, did not say hello and started going through some papers behind Tom, who was sitting in his wheelchair and did not seem to have seen her.

FAILURE TO MAINTAIN A STIMULATING ENVIRONMENT

Accompanying the need for a nurturing environment is the need for stimulation. The lack of emotional and psychological stimulation in the lives of some people was stark and painted a bleak picture of lives half lived.

Patrick found the fact that Dan was placed in the rehab facility at all to be emotionally and psychologically neglectful and even worse that he lived on the hospital side of the facility, which had two wings – a hospital side for people with more severe injury and a rehabilitation side. He felt that Dan, as a young man who was fit and healthy in so many ways, should not have spent so many years in the company of people who had been so severely brain injured that they were, in his words, 'vegetative'. He said:

> So, there was a lot of neglect, I think in that time he'd just roam the corridors, you know, chanting. He used to use it [the chant] to comfort himself, very softly and quietly.

If Patrick didn't go and visit Dan, he felt that nothing would happen for him. At one point, Patrick said he was going to see Dan every day, out of concern for his emotional and physical wellbeing. He acknowledged that staff were overworked, and that a lot of the people who lived in the facility needed a high level of care that wasn't possible for staff to provide. He felt strongly, though, that some people were better able to deal with the institutional environment, but Dan was not able to: 'shut it off and deal with it'. At one point, it became too difficult for Patrick to visit, and he stopped going to see Dan for a time, instead arranging for other people to go and read to him and so on. He said of that time:

> I reckon in the 18 months that I talked about, when I backed off, I reckon the only things they did for him were to feed him and shower him. And that's my, I mean, I wasn't there, but that's my reading of what happened.

CONNECTION BETWEEN PHYSICAL AND EMOTIONAL NEGLECT

Tom's mum, Penny, makes the connection between physical neglect and emotional neglect. She remembered going to see Tom for holidays, and spending days cleaning his house, as it was in such a filthy state when she arrived. She said, for example, the griller tray was cemented to the oven because it hadn't been cleaned for such a long time. Penny said workers do not provide food that is to Tom's tastes, and she feels he has little choice in what he eats. Tom says that he has choice and control over who works with him, and what they do, but Penny's view is that: 'You'd think Tom was working for them, rather than those workers working for him.'

While Jill was having a lot of casual staff, Ivy suspects she had some sort of choking episode, which resulted in her not being able to eat at all for days. She is still not able to chew any food at all and now has pureed food. According to Ivy, speech pathologists say this is common after someone has a severe choking episode, as it is so frightening.

LACK OF ADEQUATE CONCERN FOR WELLBEING

When Jill was left at the regional fair on her own (see p.89), the refusal of the institution doctors to check on her return that she hadn't come to physical harm, despite repeated requests, is indicative of a lack of concern for wellbeing that was demonstrated in several instances.

Ann, Jim, Fran, and Dan also experienced preventable injuries. The responses to their injuries varied, but in all case were less than vigorous or concerned. Jim, for instance, recalled being 'in trouble' when his leg was badly burned on a bus exhaust, despite the fact that he uses a wheelchair and a staff member would have had to move the chair so his leg was against the exhaust.

Compounding neglect

Ann's memory of seeking help from her mental health case worker to escape the regular fights and other abuses happening at the hostel is an example of compounding emotional and psychological neglect. Already living in an environment in which her openly stated need for emotional nurturing and sustenance ('friends') is neglected, Ann's seeking of support from an external source is a good strategy. To be not only labelled 'manipulative', but also to have your concerns flagged to the people who have perpetrated some of the abuse before being returned to the environment in which it took place, time and time again, is both neglectful and abusive.

Gemma, Ann's current support worker, is of the view that neglect was at the foundation of the way that the hostel operated. This was at a physical level, but also at an emotional and psychological level, and played out in the snide verbal asides, ongoing withholding of contact from Ann's sister (or the threat of it), the terrorising at a physical and emotional level that happened on multiple occasions and the physical maltreatment.

Neglecting at the structural level

Patrick raised the difficult subject of the impact of improving the lives of people with disability on the lives of family members. To a greater or lesser degree, one of the reasons that the family members in the study have participated in it is because they have made some major decisions that put the abuse in the past because they have stepped outside the traditional disability service structure. However, while this has undoubted benefits in the lives of people with disability, this also has significant costs in terms of energy, time and resources on families. Patrick said:

> It's just, it horrifies me that we can do this to each other, you know? I mean, I look back on this, and for years I've struggled with this, and I used to think, 'Why did you save him, if you're not going to support him?'

The following table presents the summary features of neglect as a form of emotional and psychological abuse in the lives of participants in the study.

Table 4.7 Summary of neglecting

Individual	Systemic	Structural
• Betrayal of 'care' in interpersonal interactions	• Under-resourcing increasing the risk of abuse and neglect • Failure to maintain a nurturing environment • Failure to maintain a stimulating environment • Connection between physical and emotional neglect • Lack of adequate concern for wellbeing • Compounding neglect – neglectful and abusive responses to attempts to address neglect	• Impact on family members of sustaining decent quality of life for person • Lack of community insight into damage caused by neglect of people with intellectual disability

7 Withholding, misusing or delaying needed supports

Withholding, misusing or delaying needed supports includes:

• using medication to sedate the person for agency convenience
• ignoring equipment safety requirements
• breaking or not fixing adaptive equipment
• refusing to use or destroying communication devices

- withdrawing care or equipment to immobilise the person
- using equipment to torture the person.

This form of abuse had been experienced by five participants in the study. There were 11 separate incidents described that related to the withholding, misusing or delaying of needed disability-related supports. The themes that emerged were around chemical restraint, the refusal of needed equipment and the withdrawal of needed equipment to immobilise the person.

During the interviews, participants described several other incidents of this sort of abuse that had happened to people they knew, and while they are not detailed here, they may give an indication that this form of abuse could be more common than first thought.

Withholding, misusing or delaying needed supports at the individual level

Tom had hurt his leg and called his mother for advice. She suggested that he go to the hospital and get it checked. The support worker who was working with Tom that day said 'Oh, I'm going home in a minute, I haven't got time to take you there,' and pulled all the wires out of Tom's wheelchair, so he was unable to go. The worker left, leaving Tom lying on the floor, unable to leave the house. Tom said: 'He was training to be a doctor! And I told him his bedside manner…sucked big time!'

Tom's mum, Penny, said that the worker left the organisation, but was not disciplined, as far as she was aware.

Withholding, misusing or delaying needed supports at the systemic level

CHEMICAL RESTRAINT

Jill and Dan both experienced over-medication and its serious consequences. Their stories are alarming and have both physical and emotional abuse components.

When Jill lived in the institution, her weight dropped to alarmingly low levels – 25kg at the lowest point. Her mother, Ivy, feels this was due to over-medication and a combination of heavy duty drugs, which may have not been necessary (see 'Minimising, justifying and blaming', p.86). She said: 'I always said she lived a life of misery and neglect, because your weight doesn't drop to 25 kilograms if you're being well cared for, does it?'

When Dan first moved into the rehab hospital, he used to walk independently, although he would have falls. He used to push other residents around the facility in their wheelchairs. Patrick recalled that:

> With the change of management, came a much stronger drug regime, and all of a sudden he was falling over all the time, so we've got to put him in a wheelchair. And in amongst this he was also part of a singing group that they had there. So he was so drugged out of his brain that he couldn't participate in that any more.

Patrick obtained a copy of Dan's medical records and found that Dan was on extremely high doses of anti-epilepsy and psychotropic drugs, all at the same time – apparently an unusually high volume and combination of drugs. When he questioned the staff about Dan's lack of coordination and mental functioning, he said: 'and that was the other thing they would say, "Oh, it's just natural deterioration." Oh, well how come he naturally un-deteriorates [off the medication]?'

REFUSING TO PROVIDE NEEDED EQUIPMENT

The use of the term 'equipment' here refers to any service or equipment that a person may need as a consequence of their disability. These are examples where there is not simply a failure to provide equipment, but an active refusal on the part of staff and services to provide equipment that would assist people to live more comfortably or safely.

Ivy is of the view that Jill's weight loss was also due to a refusal on the part of the institution to puree Jill's food. Jill has a swallowing disorder that makes it very difficult for her to eat. Following a choking incident she became wary of swallowing food. After Ivy consulted a speech pathologist who diagnosed oral stage dysphagia, she began pureeing all her food, and Jill finally began eating again. She has now regained weight and is much healthier.

When Tom lived in a hostel in the inner city, he lived up a flight of stairs. The hostel did not have wheelchair access, and Tom could only get in or out of the building if other residents or the owner or staff were prepared to carry him and his electric wheelchair up or down the stairs.

The assumptions that were made about Dan were very frustrating to Patrick, as he found them to be limiting and demeaning. The refusal of the manager of the facility to provide therapy to Dan, saying that it would not be 'worthwhile', mentioned earlier in the chapter, is also a clear example of emotional and psychological abuse in this category.

When Ann was coming out of the shower, she tripped over a rug and fell and broke her hip. Instead of seeking appropriate medical attention and calling an ambulance, the brother of the owner of the hostel in which she lived piggybacked her to his car and drove her to casualty.

WITHDRAWING EQUIPMENT TO IMMOBILISE THE PERSON

Three people had experienced the deliberate removal of their wheelchairs in order to prevent them from moving around their homes and communities.

Patrick used to pay a lady to go and read to Dan, when he couldn't visit himself. One day when she arrived, she found Dan in his room, where he had been put: 'like a naughty boy,' and his wheelchair taken away as a punishment. She wrote a letter outlining the circumstances, which Patrick took to the Health Minister, but unfortunately little was achieved.

Jim was punished by staff in two different facilities when his stoma bag came off. In one institution, he was smacked as a young child by a night nurse whenever his bag came off. In another hostel, he was put to bed without dinner whenever he came home from school and his bag had come off. Once Jim had been put to bed, he could not reach his wheelchair and get into it on his own, so he had to remain in bed until staff would get him up the following morning.

The table below contains the summative primary themes that emerged from the results in this area of withholding, misusing or delaying needed supports.

Table 4.8 Summary of withholding, misusing or delaying needed supports

Individual	Systemic	Structural
• Withholding equipment to immobilise the person	• Chemical restraint • Refusing to provide needed equipment • Withdrawing equipment to immobilise the person	

8 Corrupting/exploiting

Corrupting and exploiting includes:

- socialising a person into accepting ideas or behaviour that oppose legal standards
- using a person for advantage or profit
- training a person to serve the interests of the abuser.

Stories that related to five experiences of corrupting or exploiting abuse were shared by participants, centring on three different people with intellectual disability. This represents a small but important theme in the study, centring on the misuse of power by workers to require people living in services to behave in ways that they ordinarily would not – by being manipulated into malicious political staff campaigns, living routines that minimise staff workload, working as staff would (or should) or listening to confessions they would rather not hear.

Corrupting and exploiting at the individual level

Jim talked about his difficulties with a worker who was engaged to take him to and from a training provider, where he was going to learn literacy and computer skills. He said he had trouble with the worker, because she talked at great length and in great detail about her personal money troubles and unburdened herself to him about the recent death of her mother. While this is not abusive by itself, Jim was very uncomfortable with the conversation, and he gave the impression that it continued for several weeks. The inappropriateness of the worker using Jim as a 'listening ear' when his communication impairment and his lack of assertiveness dictate that he would almost certainly be unable to ask her not to talk about these issues, certainly in the level of detail that she did, changes the context of the interaction, making it an exploitative interaction due to the intensity and the one-sidedness of the communication and Jim's inability to end or leave the conversation.

Corrupting and exploiting at the systemic level

Rose felt that Jenny's friend and co-resident Ian was corrupted by male staff who worked in the group home that they shared (see 'Isolating', p.100). Not only was the longstanding relationship between Jenny and Ian damaged beyond repair, but Rose was concerned that Ian's conception of women was badly damaged and his relationship with female staff difficult. Jenny was subjected to two years of the emotional and psychological effects of being denigrated and put down by both her friend and staff who were paid to support them, and she ultimately left the accommodation service as a response to what Rose found to be an intolerable situation.

On a lower, but more chronic, level Rose talked about the way that she sometimes saw staff manage Jenny in several of the places in which she has lived, by: 'getting Jenny to be quiet, or to go to her room, or to do stuff that they want done, so it makes their job easier.'

For about 18 months Tom lived in a group home with people who had higher support needs than him. He paints a vivid picture of a lifestyle where he undertook a large proportion of household tasks, including assisting other residents to get dressed (despite having a significant physical impairment himself), teaching household tasks to other residents and cooking meals for the group. He said staff did some tasks but also watched a lot of television. Tom remembered one day when he hit breaking point:

Tom: Yeah. One day I forgot that I put a chicken in the convection microwave, and when I went back there, it had broken.

Sally: Oh no!

Tom: And it was, how can I watch and look after these lot and do that at the same time?

Sally: And what did they [staff] say?

Tom: Oh, you can do it, you know how to cook.

Tom's mum, Penny, also raised this point, saying independently of Tom that in some of the places that Tom has lived: 'You'd think Tom was working for them, rather than those workers working for him.'

The following table contains a summary of the abuse experienced in the category of corrupting and exploiting, as related by participants in their narratives.

Table 4.9 Summary of corrupting and exploiting

Individual	Systemic	Structural
• Workers emotionally offloading to residents • Sexually exploitative relationships	• Intentionally damaging relationships between co-residents • Requiring residents to complete staff duties	• Blurred roles and responsibilities

Other forms of abuse experienced

A high volume of other forms of abuse and neglect were also described by people in the course of their narratives. The following table details these abuses.

There is overlap between these abuses and the emotional and psychological abuse and neglect detailed above. Where participants talked about the emotional or psychological component to the abuse (for example, 'he feels like he can't trust men now'), the incidents have also been included in the emotional and psychological abuse categories. It is difficult to separate the causes, experience and effects of abuse and neglect, as many (if not all) forms of abuse and neglect have an emotional and psychological component. For this reason, statistical comparison is not helpful. However, what can be clearly seen from the table is that a high volume of abuses have been experienced by this small group of people.

While this study does not focus on abuses other than emotional and psychological, it would be remiss not to include mention of these other forms of maltreatment. Some of the abuses that are not fully detailed in the discussion of emotional and psychological abuse and neglect but have significant implications for the emotional health and wellbeing of people, include sexual and physical assault, witnessing the assault of others and false imprisonment in particular.

Table 4.10 Other forms of abuse
(ordered by frequency of experience)

Type of abuse/crime	Number of references in the interview data	Number of participants experiencing this form of abuse/crime
Physical neglect	26	8
Negligence (inattentive care resulting in harm)	20	7
Incompatibility with co-residents resulting in harm	15	7
Financial abuse	7	6
Failure to adequately maintain health	16	5
Physical assault	15	5
Witnessing abuse/assault of others	10	5
Assault by co-residents*	7	3
Chemical restraint	5	3
False imprisonment	8	3
Inadequate staffing resulting in harm	5	3
Theft	12	3
Injury with unknown cause	6	2
Sexual assault	4	2

Note: this total is included in physical assault but also included as a separate category to show the experience of assault by co-residents experienced by a significant number of participants.

Abuses at the individual level

The abuses that were situated in the individual domain were primarily those caused by other residents. This was mostly physical assault and was linked in several instances to systemic failures to house co-residents more appropriately so that their needs were better matched or to respond to earlier complaints about the behaviour of violent co-residents. In the cases of Fran and Jill, some injuries they received in the institution were of unknown origin, and their families assume they were received either by accident or from another resident. Three people had their possessions stolen by support workers. Two people were sexually assaulted by workers in services.

Abuses at the systemic level

Abuses with systemic cause were strongly linked to support workers and management of services. People with high support needs came to harm in several cases due to the failure of workers to maintain adequate care standards. The health of five people was damaged due to the failure of their services to provide adequate health care.

Six of the nine participants in the study experienced financial mismanagement, in some cases of significant amounts of funds. False imprisonment was an experience related by three people, where the link between the punishment of exclusionary time out and the misdeed was unclear in their minds. Chemical restraint was a long-term experience for three people.

Abuses at the structural level

The inability of people to move away from co-residents who had threatened them, or who they were frightened of, before or after they were assaulted is indicative of a structural abuse. The resulting harm to people from assaults by co-residents can be seen in part as a result of the structure of disability services systems that house groups of people with diverse support needs together without recourse to moving if the need arises.

Physical neglect was experienced by eight of the nine participants. This was expressed through the presence of preventable illnesses and injuries, such as scabies, bedsores and being underweight, provision of poor-quality food, poor medical care and unhygienic home conditions. Participants described people with high support needs living with staffing ratios of 1:6 and at times even 1:12. This is linked to the fact that three people came to harm directly as a result of inadequate staffing levels. Under-resourcing was described by several family participants as chronic and of great concern to them. The failure to provide adequate staff to support people with high support needs provided conditions ripe for abuse to occur.

This long chapter details a disturbing and distressing set of experiences. Taken separately, each person's story of emotional and psychological abuse and neglect is important for the light it sheds on the length, range and diversity of harms that individual people have experienced. Collectively, these narratives provide us with some critical insights into the implications of these shared harms for better understanding and responding to this abuse and neglect in the lives of people with intellectual disability. The following chapter takes up some of these issues at a systemic level, adding the perspectives of key policy, advocacy and service provider stakeholders.

Chapter 5

Systemic Concerns

This chapter presents the systemic contributions of advocates, service providers and policy makers about the causes, influences and responses to this harm.

Sixteen people from a range of policy perspectives participated in ten individual and small-group interviews, in order to develop a picture of the view in the state disability community about how this form of abuse and neglect is understood, how prevalent it is felt to be, how well it is recognised and responded to and ideas for how it could be better prevented and people protected against it. They were predominantly people with a longstanding history of working in the disability field, both directly with people with intellectual and other disability and in policy and advocacy contexts.

There are a limited number of people working around abuse in the government and funded non-government disability sector in Australian states, and individual participants and agencies are easily identifiable. For this reason, participants are referred to as representatives of systemic policy and advocacy agencies, service provision organisations and complaints agencies, rather than their more identifiable organisational links. Individual advocates with longstanding experience also participated in this part of the research. It should be noted that, while a cross section of agencies that deal with abuse and neglect are represented here, people in these organisations were approached on the basis of their individual knowledge, background and skill.

The discussion here follows the themes addressed in each interview – namely, the understanding and definition of the abuse; its impact; its prevalence; how well it is recognised; how well it is responded to in the sector; risk factors that may increase the likelihood of its occurrence; prevention strategies; and ideas for safeguarding and protecting people with intellectual disability and influencing change.

Understanding this form of harm

Key stakeholders had a nuanced understanding of this form of abuse and neglect and drew on both their direct support and policy experience to share their insights. They also offered a range of perspectives around the way emotional and psychological abuse and neglect were defined and how definitions were used. Themes that emerged from this part of the interviews centred on the subtlety of this form of abuse and neglect, the influence of culture and power and issues of defining this abuse and neglect.

Stakeholders who had worked with hundreds of people with intellectual disability talked about the subtle nature of emotional and psychological abuse and how it was not understood as abuse. Individual advocates recalled many examples of abuses disguised as policy, such as Therese's memory of the rule within an institution that any new resident who showed grief or tears could not have visitors until they stopped, as it was seen as better for them to get over the grieving process before seeing their family, or Kate's current experience of volunteer work in a large residential setting where all residents are fed pureed food, which is all mixed together, despite some people being able to chew food and all being able to enjoy different flavours.

Lived experience and personal perception

Heather, who has a long history in service provision and policy development, contended that service providers are not able to fully understand the experience of emotional and psychological abuse and neglect, because they don't have the life experience of living with an intellectual disability in this society. The best they can do is to sit beside people and say: 'This is my perspective. What is yours?' and 'what do we need to do to move forward?'

Brian, a systemic policy and advocacy officer, expressed the view that: 'it's probably a slippery thing. 'Cause emotional stuff is more subtle than a slap or, you know, sexual assault…what one person might consider to be emotional assault or psychological, another person might not.'

He went on to say that this subtlety may be particularly difficult for people with intellectual or cognitive disability, who may not understand why the abuse has upset them, and that there is an increased likelihood that the frustration that comes from this would be expressed through challenging behaviour.

The influence of culture and power

Therese's view of emotional and psychological abuse was that it usually happens over a long period of time and that it is part of the fabric of the system that people live in. Their lack of normative life experiences means that people have little to compare their experiences to and it is difficult for them to understand that their treatment may be abusive. Her experience was that people develop particular ways of responding to this treatment, however, and these anti-social behaviours are then treated as a problem. This then gives rise to different ways of treating people – ways in which they are treated as not quite human. Therese said:

> they're placed in situations where the expectations of how they live and what happens to them are very different to what happens for other people. And it's not until they have a different experience that they really understand that they have been abused and neglected.

Representatives of systemic policy and advocacy bodies shared the view of individual advocates that emotional and psychological abuse and neglect were fundamentally linked to the culture of services. Leanne said: 'I think that there's a culture. I think the culture, that people within the culture don't accept it exists. When you're outside it you can see that it exists, and that it's powerful.'

For Zoe, an individual advocate, the abuse of power and trust was integral to an understanding of emotional and psychological abuse and neglect. This was supported by comments by others from systemic policy and advocacy bodies. Rachael, a service provider and leader in the field, described this as an exaggeration of the power imbalance that exists between workers and clients and stressed its ongoing and growing nature. The series of incidents together influence the construction of people's identity and determine how they act in a situation. She said: 'Like people would describe feeling small, and not listened to, not being heard. Or they have a disagreement, and feel the disagreement was not being an equal playing field, it escalated into something else where they were blamed disproportionately.'

Defining abuse and neglect

Polly was a representative of a systemic policy and advocacy body, but her understanding of emotional and psychological abuse was also built from her earlier experience as a service provider. She conceived of it as quite subtle in many cases, and involving behaviours such as treating people as objects, not respecting their basic humanity and right to dignity and ignoring their emotional needs and the need for connection. She recalled instances of seeing people speaking to and treating people with disability roughly, threatening people, taking away treasured possessions or activities without reason, ridiculing people and denying people opportunities to develop self-esteem and the experience of achievement because the worker wants to get things done. Polly also felt that:

> some people are quite resilient to that, and some are not, and some people will internalise it to a greater degree and it affects their life experience to a greater degree. And it's very hard to identify unless you are spending a lot of time with people.

Heather, who has a long history in both service provision and disability services policy, understood emotional and psychological abuse as any behaviour or action that is inconsistent with treating someone as a valued person and as someone with dignity. Others identified some unusual features of this form of abuse. Charlie, an individual advocate, talked about some more subtle put-downs that people experienced, such as the friendly banter that frequently exists between staff, but often not between staff and residents. Robyn, a systemic advocate, raised the failure of services to support people with intellectual disability through their grief in times of loss, such as the death of family members.

A systemic policy and advocacy body that is charged with protecting people with disability from abuse and neglect did not use a definition of emotional and psychological abuse in its practice, or perceive a need for it, as it saw its role as to: 'enquire into function'; neither did a systemic advocacy programme that spent a lot of time in disability services, considering its role to be to look at individual issues and then consider whether abuse or neglect might explain the circumstances – it was felt more appropriate to use the broadest definition possible of 'abuse, neglect or exploitation'. Leanne, the representative of this organisation, was at pains to point out that this did not mean ignoring indicators of emotional or psychological abuse but that it was not the role of an individual advocate to assess this, rather to identify issues of concern and raise the alert for further investigation.

Emotional and psychological neglect was raised as an issue of concern by several stakeholders. Polly argued that neglect was a form of abuse and that most people living in disability services were emotionally neglected. She defined this neglect as: 'failure to treat the person's aspirations, goals and dreams, and on the other side of that of course would be their sorrows and hurts'. The sorts of failures to act that she saw were in the isolation of residents, the lack of assistance provided to people to have meaningful relationships with others, the lack of assistance to be able to communicate with others, the neglect of health and responding to a person's frustration and anger without respecting the cause of it, so that the person's frustration increases. She pointed out that with a ratio of one staff member to five residents in a group home, it is not possible to achieve these things. Others identified the failure of the service system to stimulate people with disability, particularly those with autism, as neglect.

The multifaceted understanding of stakeholders about this form of abuse and neglect was both complex and sophisticated. The cultural, interpersonal and interrelational aspects raised highlight the complex nature of this form of maltreatment and raise questions about the benefits of sharing understandings of emotional and psychological abuse and neglect.

Impact

The impact of emotional and psychological abuse on people with intellectual disability was seen by stakeholders to be profound. The subtlety of comments made by workers, both verbally and in progress notes, combined with the difficulties that people have in identifying such abuses and raising them as concerns, was seen to result in an abrading or degrading of the person's psyche – what Adam, a representative of a systemic policy and advocacy body, referred to as a 'wearing effect'. Carol, his colleague, put it this way:

They are already disabled, and they become infinitely more disabled…
they are unable to self-actuate because at a fundamental level they
are being hurt, in their very heart and inner lives, which people don't
see, and they don't address. So, I think that the impact's huge.

Leanne, a representative of a systemic advocacy programme, talked about
the concerning trend of residents isolating themselves in their bedrooms
in response to violence between residents and what they termed 'staffing
arrangements'. She and others also identified a lack of recognition on
the part of staff that witnessing violence was, in itself, emotionally and
psychologically damaging. Robyn, from another agency, also talked
about the range of abuses that can accompany inappropriate matching
of co-residents. Leanne said: 'So, while no-one comes up to [us] and
says, "I'm being emotionally abused," certainly the [advocates] visiting
sites are affected by what they see. It's the impact of what people are
hearing and seeing, on each other.'

Individual advocates provided many examples of emotional and
psychological abuse and neglect that had occurred in the lives of
people they supported. Therese's view that: 'they talk about it still, so it
obviously affects them still' was representative of the attitude of all four
individual advocates about the impact of the abuse. Complaints services
commented that the abuse increased anxiety, sometimes dramatically, in
people who may already have difficulties managing anxiety.

The impact for families was also raised, both in terms of the emotional
strain of being concerned for the safety of their family member, but
also in terms of the delicate balance that needs to be maintained with
services, so that they don't become 'troublesome' parents, who complain
too much, because that will have implications for their son or daughter
once complaints and monitoring agencies have gone.

Another strong theme that emerged here was around the cauterising
or cutting off of relationships between people with intellectual disability
and support workers by services, where the decision is made by
management to move a staff member on to another house, because a
resident is becoming attached to them. Several key stakeholders raised
this as a concerning feature of service provision, and one that they saw
as emotionally and psychologically abusive. Several examples were
given where staff had been moved and residents were not provided with
the opportunity to say goodbye to them. It is a difficult relationship
to navigate, as there is a need for some boundaries. However, the grief

caused by poor management of such important relationships is abusive and cruel, and was seen to have a sometimes devastating impact on residents. The poverty of the emotional lives of people who live solely within disability services was starkly pointed out by Dagmar, in saying: 'It must be horrible to have no-one who loves you.'

Heather was troubled by the fact that people with disability she knew hadn't reacted to and fought against emotional and psychological abuse, when she would have expected them to, out of fear of a loss of service. She had watched them trade off their dignity and their right to be free from abuse in order to receive a service. She said: 'So, when I look at those people, who are among probably the least vulnerable of people with disability, and if that's their experience, and that's the impact for them, then I hate to think what it means for others.'

Prevalence

The shared contention of all stakeholders was that the rate of emotional and psychological abuse and neglect experienced by people living in disability accommodation services was high, certainly far higher than any existing figures would show and, in Heather's words: 'prevalent enough to warrant significantly more comprehensive services than we currently have'.

The complaints referral service advised that in their 2007 annual report, psychological abuse accounted for 27 per cent of all abuses notified to their service nationally. The manager said these figures may not be very reliable, given that systemic abuse is also highly rated in their figures, and their reported difficulty in determining whether abuse is primarily emotional/psychological or systemic in cause.

Carol, representing a systemic policy and advocacy body, said that their agency is of the view that the level of emotional and psychological abuse of people with intellectual disability is quite high. She talked about the difficulties in looking at changes in a person's behaviour to gauge emotional or psychological abuse, particularly when people were not able to tell their own story, to try and overcome conflicting stories about what had occurred. She concluded: 'So, because it is such a difficult area to prove, I think we see a massive under-reporting of it on the ground, because our ability to respond to it in an appropriate way is very limited.'

Leanne, who represented a systemic policy and advocacy body that spent a lot of time in disability services, said that the level of emotional and psychological abuse and neglect in those services was: 'extreme'. She argued that people come to accept it and that it becomes acceptable because, over time, the lack of resources and training and independent scrutiny mean that a certain level of emotionally abusive and neglectful practice can become the norm. She said:

> And so it's, it doesn't strike people as being unusual or strange or unacceptable, because that's just the way it is. And that's the biggest problem, I think, and the reason why it's so prevalent. I think it's massively under-reported because that's just the way it is. There's a level of acceptance in the funding.

Recognition

Stakeholders discussed recognition of emotional and psychological abuse and neglect in differing ways. Complaints response agencies detailed their processes for receiving and acknowledging complaints about abuse, while policy and advocacy bodies and individual advocates talked about systemic issues they had encountered in disability services concerning the way that emotional and psychological abuse and neglect are recognised among workers and managers and by people with intellectual disability themselves. These centred on recognition by workers and recognition by the service system.

Overlaying the discussions about recognition was the view of most stakeholders that many people with intellectual disability may not realise that what is happening to them is in fact abuse.

Lack of recognition by workers

When Charlie worked for a large disability service, he was involved in the development of their abuse policy. It included emotional abuse and neglect but he said it was rarely reported, as workers did not observe or identify it sufficiently well to report it.

Other stakeholders also raised the issue of staff at times not recognising emotional and psychological abuse and the example was given of staff not understanding the impact on residents of witnessing violence between other residents. Zoe discussed the ease with which workers could be drawn into cultures that were disrespectful and abusive, giving an example from her own practice in which she become acclimatised to quite dehumanised conditions in an institution within a short period of visiting there and relating how difficult she found it to keep normalising her view of what is appropriate behaviour in that context.

Polly, representing the view of her systemic policy and advocacy agency, argued that emotional and psychological abuse and neglect may be perceived as part of a person's disability by someone who does not know them well and overlooked.

Lack of recognition by the service system

Heather had worked extensively with service providers in recent times and found that they were having to focus heavily on viability concerns, leaving few of them: 'comfortable with just basic survival, [so they] can lift their sights a bit and look a bit at the bigger picture'.

Charlie also talked about the frustrations of a system that fails to consider people holistically, instead concentrating on vacancy management and funding imperatives that constrict options. He viewed the increasing corporatisation of disability services as having a significant impact on recognition of emotional and psychological abuse and neglect, and he saw the increased focus on managerial approaches, occupational health and safety and workplace standards and the concomitant drive to make best financial use of limited resources resulting in a concentration on the physical environment, at the expense of the emotional one.

Polly and her colleagues also discussed their view that neglect is not on the agenda of disability services systems at all, unless it is extreme – almost to the point of death. This was supported by the views of individual advocates, who contended that sexual and physical crimes and abuses, being much more easily identifiable, receive far greater attention, even within their own organisations.

Examples were also provided of policy at a high level that failed to consider the potentially abusive implications on people with intellectual disability. Therese recalled attending a consultation about the development of state-wide policy on abuse, neglect and assault. The draft policy did not include recognition of assault from one resident to another. She also recalled arguing over domestic violence policy with the state Housing Department, which had a policy that no-one should have to tolerate domestic violence. This policy does not extend to resident-to-resident assault in group homes.

Complaints

Complaints agencies discussed their systems for recording complaints about emotional and psychological abuse and neglect. In both cases, they are allocated a particular 'box' in a database, sometimes multiple categories, depending on the particular situation. One agency participating in the research was a referral agency and stressed that recognition of particular forms of abuse did not change the action they took, which remained the same in all cases. However, the recognition of particular forms of abuse is reflected in their annual reports and other public material, which helps to establish prevalence. The other agency was a resolution and prevention body and matched particular portions of complaints against a matrix of definitions developed from the state government Disability Services Standards. These are fairly general on abuse, using a broad definition, although the operational policy guidelines used by the agency include emotional abuse. This agency raised a difference in recognition between themselves and the other agency, which centred on systemic and emotional abuse.

The referral complaints agency recognised abuse that had at its root organisationally or policy-driven causes as systemic abuse (and as other forms of abuse at the same time too, depending on the circumstance). Examples given were of all residents of a group home being put into their pyjamas by seven o'clock and all residents having to eat the same menu without choice. The prevention and response complaints agency did not include recognition of systemic abuse in its policy and would instead record these sorts of experiences as examples of emotional abuse, contending that regardless of the intention of the service, the experience for the client is still emotionally abusive. However, some of the examples they provided indicated a preference to address issues as questions of lack of choice or failure to have individual needs addressed, rather than questions of possible abuse. The agency indicated that they would classify the allegation into the category in which they were most likely to get a clear-cut recommendation for change at the end of an investigation process.

Response

Stakeholders provided perspectives on a range of responses that were given to people when they experienced emotional and psychological abuse, which covered a continuum from effective and appropriate concern through to bizarre reactions that amplified the impact of the initial abuse. Complaints agencies detailed their processes for responding to complaints about this form of maltreatment and the sorts of outcomes that people could commonly expect in these situations.

The impact of policy on responses to abuse

Systemic policy and advocacy agencies discussed the response that they sometimes received from services regarding concerns about abuse, that: 'We're fine, we've got a policy to cover that.' They expressed concern that the link between having the policy and implementing the policy did not appear to be made in some cases, nor did the necessary accompanying actions such as training staff, informing clients and families of the policy and so on.

When Charlie worked for a large disability service provider, the most frequently reported abuses in that organisation were physical assaults. While it was not identified as such, Charlie saw a strong current of emotional and psychological abuse also running through these reports. When a pattern of incidents was identified, a person would sometimes be moved to another house, using a vacancy management system. Charlie felt that most of these would not have occurred if more appropriate accommodation and an emotional and psychological support framework had been in place.

Fears were expressed by several stakeholders that new regulations governing the use of restrictive practices would give the 'green light' to services to use behaviour management strategies, such as restraint, exclusionary time out and sedative medication, far more frequently in response to challenging behaviour by residents. Their concern arose from two points – that the restrictive practices may cause emotional harm, and that the challenging behaviour may be in response to emotional or other abuse, restrictive practices being a most inappropriate response to it.

Double standards

The standards of protection that were offered to staff and to residents when faced with violent residents in some cases differed widely. Individual advocates raised examples of instances when staff had been assaulted by residents – they received counselling, stress leave and double-up shifts. However, when residents were assaulted by the same resident, they did not receive anything. Therese said:

They even employed an extra worker in, I think they've got an extra worker in five houses in [government run service], just to support the staff, because the houses were so abusive, and yet the abuse was usually targeted to another person with a disability.

Criminal history checks are conducted on staff but no similar checks on clients, and very vulnerable people with intellectual disability may have to live in the same house as someone with a strong history of violence. This also cuts the other way, with some people labelled as extremely challenging due to a single incident that occurred years ago, which follows them, out of context, and taints their associations with staff and fellow residents through house after house.

Responses of complaints agencies

The complaints bodies responded to complaints about emotional and psychological abuse and neglect in differing ways. The referral agency took details from individual complaints over the phone or in writing and referred the matter to agencies in each state for resolution. The resolution and prevention agency took complaints either verbally or in writing and then broke them into what they called 'workable chunks', allocated a risk level to the allegation and conducted an investigation into the veracity of the complaint.

From here, the aim of the agency was to resolve the complaint in a collaborative manner and, ultimately, to reconcile the client and service. It should be noted that complaints about criminal matters are referred on to another agency. Three reports are generated from complaints – at the client, operational and strategic levels. The first contains recommendations aimed at resolving the specific complaint, the second contains issues pertinent to the local support system, such as training or regional support, and the strategic report relates to whole-of-programme concerns for the state.

In response to questions about how the agency responds to the subtlety of emotional and psychological abuse, and the lack of 'hard evidence' of this abuse, Andrea and Dagmar pointed to the perceived benefit for the complainant of having the worker realise that their actions were seen to be abusive, even though it cannot be proven that they were so. They also said they often recommended staff training and, on occasion, for letters of acknowledgement and apology for the distress caused to be sent to the person. Dagmar said:

So sometimes, the best that we can achieve is to give the person that lodged the complaint a full and thorough explanation of what really did happen [sic]. Maybe because information hadn't been kept, or hadn't been provided back, and where you don't have information, you tend to fill in the gaps for yourself, and then you're going off on assumptions. So, most of the complaints are really about a breakdown in communication.

Risk factors

Systemic policy and advocacy bodies saw the risk of emotional and psychological abuse and neglect being increased by a number of factors, including the history of violence in some services, the impact on the environment of under-resourcing, the staffing arrangements, lack of knowledge and understanding of people and abuse between residents. Leanne's view was that the combination of factors was: 'just like a flourishing little hot bed for it to happen'.

The place of services in people's lives was seen to be important in terms of risk. The lack of relationships external to services – informal relationships, friendships and family connections – was viewed as a significant risk factor for emotional and psychological abuse and neglect by most key stakeholders. Complaints agencies reported receiving few complaints from people with intellectual disability, saying they received most of their complaints from family members, advocates or other representatives of people with intellectual disability.

Intentionality of abuse

The majority of key stakeholder participants were at pains to point out their view that the bulk of emotionally and psychologically abusive and neglectful acts were not carried out with malicious intent. Rather, they were more often seen to be the result of unthinking application of rules and policies or making choices in the heat of a stressful moment that, on reflection, were not good choices. However, systemic responses to these instances at times promulgate disrespectful values and set up frameworks that fail to respect the rights of residents. Charlie gave a cogent example of this, in relating the experience of a support worker who was untrained and unsupported in a group home. Her support of a man was handled poorly, and he became loud and aggressive. The worker was hit, and in the heat of the moment, she hit him back. While Charlie did not condone this action, he understood it and placed it in a context of her lack of training, support and guidance. However, she was not disciplined, but moved to another house and provided with self-protective behaviours training. No action was taken on behalf of the resident.

Polly talked about the dysfunctionality she had witnessed in professional teams during her work history and how this creates a situation of risk for people with intellectual disability. The power conflicts that she saw arise on a number of occasions played out in a range of ways, including resistance to involving families in the lives of the person with intellectual disability. She recalled support teams trying to limit the involvement of families in birthday and Christmas parties and other token occasions, rather than inviting them to be involved in individual planning meetings and weekend activities or routinely seeking their engagement.

Risk increased by broad disability policy

The funding imperative that forces the shared housing of people with intellectual disability was seen by some stakeholders to be a risk factor for emotional and psychological abuse and neglect. If a person requires a high level of support, it is common that in order to obtain adequate staffing support they need to pool their funds with another person and share support by living together. In practice, this frequently results in three or four people sharing a group home, with little recourse for movement in or out, as each resident is dependent on the funds of the others. Vacancies in group homes are managed on a database by the state disability department, and individual advocates noted that people with significant intellectual disability are, in their experiences, the most likely to be co-housed with people with severe challenging behaviour, as they have someone else making their decisions. They don't have the problem-solving skills to keep themselves safe, to navigate relationships or to move to another living situation if they are unhappy.

The introduction of new regulations on the use of restrictive behaviour management practices, such as restraint and seclusion, had recently occurred at the time of interview and was fresh in people's minds. Both individual advocates and systemic policy and advocacy bodies expressed concerns about the link between restrictive practices and emotional and psychological abuse, particularly the fact that guidelines providing clarity around the use of these techniques may also condone and legitimise their use. This is even more strongly the case where safeguards are seen to be weak. In a climate of under-resourcing and under-skilling of workers, it was viewed as likely that restrictive practices will be used more often than ideal, and they will no doubt have a strong emotional and psychological impact.

Charlie saw the failure of the service system to link people with intellectual disability to workers who knew them well and who could support them emotionally as neglectful and abusive. The high rates of casual staffing used in the field mean that people are frequently supported by strangers in their daily lives, including for their intimate personal care and emotional needs. Charlie said:

> And that's such the vulnerability of people with disabilities, is that they are ultimately vulnerable to the person who walks through the door for the next eight hours. And it shouldn't be, they should be able to expect a standard of, quality of, reflective practice, and that just doesn't happen.

The increasing compliance culture of the service system was seen by some stakeholders to be a risk factor for abuse. Rachael expressed it well, in saying:

> I think we've created an environment where individuals working in the system, whether they be paid or unpaid, are less inclined to trust their own judgement than they are to check what rule applies here. I think that's a dangerous thing for people.

One representative of a systemic policy and advocacy body argued that government funding agencies responsible for the accommodation and support of people with intellectual disability needed to face some hard truths. With hundreds, if not thousands, of people waiting for services and budgets that are significantly short of where they need to be in order to support existing clientele, departments are forced into a harm-minimisation approach in the way they manage clients. Brian asserted that:

> what we need is some recognition that this forces some deliberate risks, let's work on identifying those, let's put in place some strategies to minimise the harm. In saying that I'm not advocating that people should be lumped together in bad situations with tenants they're not

compatible with, but the reality is that, in the current context, they will be. So, being pragmatic and realising well, that's the world we live in at this point in time, what can we do to minimise the harm that comes to people?

Protection and safeguards

A number of stakeholders raised the fact that, before it can be addressed, there is a need for acknowledgement of the fact that emotional and psychological abuse and neglect are happening to people with intellectual disability in disability services. This needs to happen at the broadest social level, as well as within disability services. There was seen to be little public demand for emotional and psychological abuse and neglect to be addressed. Although there is a certain level of abhorrence around sexual assault of people with disability, as Carol put it: 'as for the rest, it's so far under the radar that there's no leverage externally to say, you know, hang on a minute.'

Adam linked safeguards with the need for clear and unambiguous definitions of emotional and psychological abuse and neglect, which leave people in no doubt about what constitutes such maltreatment – saying that the need for protection from this form of abuse would reduce with an increased knowledge about what constitutes it, given that it is perpetrated out of ignorance rather than malice in many instances.

International human rights instruments were viewed by some stakeholders as a useful framework within which to gauge the degree to which the lives of people with intellectual disability living in disability accommodation services met basic human rights standards.

Protection from retaliation and retribution for making a complaint about abuse was raised as an area that is currently not well addressed. Within current quality assurance systems, service providers are required to ensure that residents are protected from retribution if they make a complaint, but according to systemic policy and advocacy bodies, those mechanisms are flimsy. Brian expressed his lack of confidence that these mechanisms would protect people against emotional and psychological abuse and neglect, saying: 'There's a thousand ways to emotionally abuse someone, and most of them quite subtle.'

Relationships external to services

Stakeholders consistently put forward the view that one of the strongest safeguards for people with intellectual disability lay in keeping them connected in their relationships, and that relationships with people who know you well and value you as an individual have a powerful protective function. A key role for service providers was seen as supporting and developing these relationships, in this context as a safeguarding measure against abuse.

Several stakeholders identified the need for substantially more independent advocacy support for people with intellectual disability in order to address emotional and psychological abuse and neglect in their lives. In addition to ongoing advocacy, they saw a need for independent support for people to make complaints and to walk alongside them throughout the complaints process. The current systems offer little ongoing support – one purely by phone and the other with limited contact. The barriers for people with intellectual disability to make complaints themselves are high, and complaints agencies reported receiving few complaints directly from them. Rachael pointed out that in order for advocacy support to be effective, resources need to be in place to allow for quick resolution of problems, in a non adversarial way, to best meet the needs of all parties. Heather's belief was that: 'the prevalence is such that we should feel very embarrassed about the level of support we offer.'

Community-based and individualised environments

Key stakeholders were consistent in their responses that individually oriented, community-based living arrangements were protective for people with intellectual disability. Their increased presence in their community, and the larger number of incidental relationships they formed while going about their daily lives, form natural safeguards against abuse. Some individual advocates also saw small, family-driven, holistic services that viewed the person as more than a client were a strong protective agent.

Scrutiny of services

Several stakeholders identified a need for better valuing of external scrutiny and for checks and balances that address this culture and draw the attention of workers and managers to the effects of cultural influences that subtly degrade and disrespect the rights of residents. In order for this to be effective, a shift needs to occur to allow for reflective learning and understanding of relationships, interactions and values – and a focus predominantly on residents, rather than service management.

The resolution and prevention complaints body representative, Andrea, talked about the role their agency played in leveraging change in services through recommending changes as a result of involvement in compliance auditing processes. Some of these recommendations were around training for staff, ensuring that staff were aware of particular policies and procedures and so on. There is also some capacity for the agency to recommend increased resources, where systemic practices are the root cause of people's abuse.

Tensions in the funder/provider role of government were raised by stakeholders as complex and at times contradictory. Governments in Australia are both funders and providers of services, contracting out services to many non-government organisations as well as providing accommodation support directly in several states. Complaints and monitoring functions are administratively separated from service provision, but those sections report to senior management who maintain overall responsibility for the operation of the Department.

Training, education and support for workers

Training and education were raised by stakeholders as important tools in protecting people from abuse and neglect. Training and education were discussed on several levels, including attitudes and values-based education, rights-based training and practice-based training. Complaints bodies conduct training and also recommend training and education as primary outcomes of complaints resolution processes. This training is geared to particular issues, such as how to make a complaint, behaviour management or individual planning. They viewed this training as important for both complaint response and also as a tool in their prevention role. One of the systemic policy and advocacy bodies identified the need for training and support for families to identify emotional and psychological abuse or, perhaps more supportively, to identify the signs that their family member is satisfied and what action to take if they don't believe their family member is happy in their home.

The need for better support and supervision of direct support workers was raised by a systemic policy and advocacy body. This was couched not in terms of monitoring and checking of performance, but rather encouragement, mentoring and facilitating their performance. This builds on the view of several stakeholders that much of the abuse that occurs in disability services happens out of ignorance or blind following of rules, rather than malicious intent. Heather said:

> If it's something that you, if you come into a workplace and you see it as accepted practice, and you're not as discerning as you would be in other circumstances, and you just don't see it. And if somebody is able to work with you in a way that is non judgemental, and that they can support you to see that, and that's a process of growth and people need support to do that.

Protective qualities of workers

Rachael saw the focus of service provision as being predominantly on physical care and recreation. She identified a need for emotionally mature workers who focus on working with people to develop and support their emotional capacity, and suggested that this was an area where workers needed to be better recognised and paid. While training is vital, it can only go so far in teaching emotional maturity, and workers need to come to a job with a certain amount of maturity in order to be able to adequately support people without resorting to power plays and games of ownership and 'who knows you best', which lead to emotional and psychological abuse and neglect. This was supported by comments from workers in a systemic policy and advocacy agency, who noted that some of the comments made by staff about residents that they had viewed in progress notes over time were reflective of very poor attitudes and a fundamental lack of respect, which opened the door to emotional abuse.

Individual advocates expressed the view that it was essential for individual workers to take responsibility for their own behaviour in order for real safeguarding to occur. Heather expressed the view that a legislative framework needs to be in place, and clarity of expectations around standards, but:

> that real safeguarding comes from individuals being, taking responsibility for their own behaviour, and the heavier, the bigger the stick that's held up to people, the less they take control and responsibility for their own behaviour, because you've shifted the control and the responsibility externally.

Prevention

The development and maintenance of relationships that were not reliant on the service system was raised by most stakeholders as an important factor in preventing abuse from occurring. Such relationships included friendships, family relationships and ongoing, personal advocacy relationships, such as citizen advocacy-style programmes.

The need for education and training for workers was also raised as an important prevention strategy. Rachael pinpointed the limitations of the competency-based training in this area, arguing that it does not teach workers the process work about how you get people to talk about emotions or how a worker might adapt their technique to work with people with particular emotional needs, such as people with autism or acquired brain injury. Charlie identified values-based education for direct support workers as critical, so that they can make decisions that are grounded in a framework based around the rights and needs of people with disability. He said:

> And if you can enculturate that into people who [are] at the coal face delivering support, because that's where the rubber hits the road, then that would be the most significant, broad impact you could have. So long as those values work with the relative structures they're getting from the service.

Some of the physical structures of services in this state remain anchored in the past. While large groups of people are housed together, it is very difficult to make changes that will dramatically improve people's quality of life. Kate, when asked how abuse could be prevented at the institution where she works, said: 'Nothing could make [institution] better. Not while you have 70 people living together.'

Influencing change

Key stakeholders were in a position to influence change, and one of the questions they were asked concerned this role and how they could act to influence the rates at which people experienced emotional and psychological abuse.

Individual advocates felt that there was a need to acknowledge, on the broadest level, that the lives of people with intellectual disability who live in disability services were lived in such a way that they were ripe for abuses. As Zoe phrased it:

nowhere else do people who are unrelated live in a group home, where their tenancy is decided by the government, in a lot of cases, or the service deliverer. And they live there for their life. And until that is adequately acknowledged, and what that does to people, it's…

One systemic policy and advocacy body related a success story that they felt demonstrated the benefit of developing relationships over time and the power of incremental change. In this instance, a relationship was established with a resistant service in which many allegations of abuse had been made over a long time. Instead of a confrontational approach, the agency took an approach of working alongside support workers for an extended period, using a process of facilitating, supporting and advising them on several issues, such as re-engaging people with their families. Brian commented that this worked quite positively and proved that: 'there are times for coming in with the big stick, and there are times for coming in with a different approach.'

Changing the dominant culture of disability services systems was recognised as being a highly challenging, complex and difficult undertaking. It was seen to necessitate tackling industrial issues, HR issues, occupational health and safety and a myriad of other concerns relating to the working environment. There were seen to be roles for external people to facilitate and encourage culture shift, but stakeholders were also of the view that:

> If you're doing all that externally, you still need people on the inside, and that's the hard job. You get leaders in pockets actually doing the hard work of confronting the culture. Because you can do it all from out here, you can plan it and have that strategy, but it has to happen from the inside.

The importance of having multiple points of intervention to make change to people's experience of emotional and psychological abuse and neglect was raised by a systemic policy and advocacy body. While much of this abuse has systemic roots, this group cautioned that individual people should not be forgotten and assumed to be passive victims of a systemic problem. It must also be acknowledged that a risk exists that people who are already entrenched in a systemically abusive system will be further abused if they try to challenge that abuse. With care, however, it was felt that people with intellectual disability should undoubtedly be provided with skill development opportunities to learn protective skills and strategies. There was also a need identified for different education strategies for people who have experienced abuse, people who have not and people who have not yet entered disability services systems.

The complaints bodies were of the view that they worked to influence change on both a case-by-case basis and at a strategic level. The referral body had limited capacity to influence change, apart from ensuring referrals were taken up by referral agencies. It presented regular summaries of data to its funding body but was precluded in its funding agreement from using data derived from its operations for analytic purposes, so did not publicly present or promote findings about prevalence or trends. The resolution and prevention agency argued that their conciliation approach enabled them to resolve a high proportion of complaints, as they required a low standard of proof, and could recommend any course of action that they felt would be helpful or useful to the person, the organisation or the system. In addition, they had a systemic role of preventing abuse and neglect, which they addressed through identifying trends in reporting, initiating training and education, and communicating issues of concern at a senior management, regional and state management level to leverage change on abuse issues.

The contributions of key stakeholders provide a different perspective of emotional and psychological abuse and neglect. Their systemic viewpoint opens for consideration broader issues of understanding, impact, recognition and response, risk factors, safeguarding and prevention.

PART 3

Making Change and Moving Forward

Sally: Do you still live at the place where the bad things happened?
Ann: No. But they're still in my head.

Chapter 6

What do These Experiences Mean for Other People With Intellectual Disability?

This chapter identifies and discusses some of the key issues that emerge from the research, including the diffuse and pervasive nature of this harm; damage done by thoughtless following of 'the rules' by workers; issues of control and punishment; the lack of adequate concern shown to people who were hurt; withholding of basic support and rights; and the significant impact on their lives. Finally, the chapter discusses the important place that strategies of resistance and resilience have in the lives of people who have experienced this harm.

The experiences of emotional and psychological abuse and neglect shared by individuals, families and supporters both confirm and extend the understanding of this form of abuse in previous research. Their experiences were themed against the abuse framework developed in Chapter 2. They were also categorised according to the origin of the abuse in the individual, systemic or structural domain (Penhale 1999). The use of the two frameworks together provides both a detailed picture of the individual lived experience of the abuse and also allows consideration of the individual, systemic or structural domain in which the abuse is rooted. Conclusions can be drawn from this dual framework for strategies for change to prevent and better respond to this form of abuse and neglect, which are at the same time grounded in the lived experience of people with intellectual disability and are useful in the policy context (Chapters 8 and 9).

Some new behaviours and actions emerged through this combination of lived experience and critique, which had not, to date, featured in the literature on emotional and psychological abuse and neglect. These included:

- taking away treasured possessions or activities without reason
- denying people opportunities to develop self-esteem and the experience of achievement because the worker wants to get things done
- failing to support people through grief and loss
- maintaining differential relationships (e.g., having no easy 'banter' with residents, as with co-workers)
- responding to a person's frustration and anger without respecting the cause of it, so that the person's frustration increases.

All nine people with intellectual disability experienced multiple forms of emotional and psychological abuse and neglect on multiple occasions. As detailed in Chapter 4, they were all subjected to abuse of caregiver privilege, degrading, isolating and minimising, justifying and blaming. Eight of the nine had experience of emotional neglect, and seven had been terrorised. Five people had experience of having needed disability-related supports withheld, misused or delayed and three people were emotionally corrupted or exploited.

Across this range of abuse and neglect, a number of themes emerge that apply to all or most of the categories of emotional and psychological abuse and neglect.

This discussion must, however, be prefaced by the recognition of a centrally important feature that emerges from the experiences of the narrators and that underpins this discussion. The use and misuse of power and control is ubiquitous in this experience. It provides the context within which individual experiences occur, the preconditions for interpersonal interactions and the framework for both systemic and structural injustices. The results of the research, as they have unfolded in the last two chapters, progressively reveal the centrality of power relations in this form of abuse and neglect. The critical role of power and control in understanding emotional and psychological abuse and neglect forms a foundational building block.

The diffuse and pervasive nature of the abuse

The climate that was created by the multiple abuse experiences coloured the world of the nine participants and is central to understanding their experiences of emotional and psychological abuse and neglect. The abuse they experienced was in many cases diffuse and pervasive, and it spread into all areas of their lives. This can be seen particularly clearly in the neglect of people's emotional and psychological wellbeing and the failure of services to provide emotional support, nurturance and stimulation to them. It also featured strongly in the experiences of degrading that people related, where their personal preferences, family structures and cultural connections were ridiculed, belittled and disrespected.

This theme adds to a small existing literature that recognises the creation of a climate of insult and the significant impact of ongoing, routine abuse in the lives of people with disability (Brown 2004; Horne *et al.* 2001). Much of the existing literature contains a focus on abuse incidents, and a primary focus on sexual and physical abuse and neglect of people with disability. Emotional and psychological abuse and neglect are almost a 'second tier' abuse in these studies, which do not talk about its pervasive and cumulative effects.

Damage done by thoughtless following of policy and practice by staff

A considerable amount of the abuse people experienced was due to staff 'following the rules', when the rules impacted on the dignity, autonomy and relationships of people living in the services. Fundamentally, this related to staff prioritising the benefit of the service system over the benefit of the individuals within it. This abuse included actions by staff that damaged relationships between people with intellectual disability and families by making families feel unwelcome in services, and thoughtless humiliating practices, such as Tom living with such poor physical access that he had to rely on other residents to carry him in or out of the building. Policies were also enforced in such a way that their intent was skewed. Jim's belief, for example, that he is not allowed to have a cordial relationship with any support worker who comes to his house, after being chastised by the service management for becoming friendly with a worker, has resulted in ongoing uncomfortableness, degradation and isolation in his interactions with support staff – sometimes the only people he sees in a week.

Consideration of some of the reasons that staff may 'follow the rules' to the detriment of people living in services is given in the next chapter. However, reasons for the unthinking following of policy and established practice include the dominant bio-medical conceptions of disability that frame service provision; managerial systems of care; low resourcing; and technically oriented and procedurally driven staff training that fails to adequately humanise people with intellectual disability (DiRita *et al.* 2008; White *et al.* 2003). All of these combine to create a culture in which the following of procedural process is accorded higher priority than responding to individual harms.

The abusive impact of poor-quality care

The quality of care provided to people with intellectual disability had clear ramifications for their emotional and psychological wellbeing. Ann's recollection of the humiliation of being dragged down the corridor to her room by other residents and left on the floor overnight when she couldn't get herself into bed unassisted is a clear example of these practices. The experiences of being degraded, humiliated and shamed, and blaming the person's disability for the abuse, were particularly strongly related to institutional approaches to care. These approaches centred on practices of workers and managers, rather than facilities, and although many of the practices did occur within large residential facilities, they were also experienced in group homes and small shared and individual settings.

There is a clear link here to other research on institutional abuse, particularly the work of Brown (2004, 2007) and Sobsey (1994) in recognising the inequities of power between staff and residents, the collective nature of some of the abuse, the denial or covering up of the abuse and the tacit or explicit condoning of poor practice that allows abusive and neglectful acts to continue.

Fighting for control

Having control over decisions, small and large, was a recurring problem for people. People with intellectual disability frequently described having their decision-making control taken away by support workers.

Families had serious problems getting access to information or having input into decisions about their family members' health, wellbeing and, in several cases, family members being harmed. Family members also described active processes of discrediting and delegitimising of their role and relationships by services and staff. The lack of control over both small- and large-scale issues connected directly to emotional abuses of caregiver privilege, withholding of needed supports and corrupting.

This connects directly to existing research on power relations, which holds that there is a serious imbalance of power structured into traditional disability services, which perpetuates a climate ripe for abuse (Mandeville and Hanson 2000; Wardhaugh and Wilding 1993).

Punishment

Punishment was a major theme in the research. People with intellectual disability were punished for their behaviour, both to encourage future compliance to rules and for complaining about the quality of their care. Punishment was a standard practice of a number of services, and three people with intellectual disability recalled with fear their experiences in time-out rooms. A number of family members were very aware of the subtle punishment that was meted out to their family members if they complained too vigorously about their treatment and felt they had to tread a careful line. This is also connected to the literature on power relations, detailed above.

Damage to relationships

Service policies and practices damaged the relationships between people with intellectual disability and those who were important in their lives. Less commonly, relationships were deliberately damaged by the actions of individual support workers. This happened in several ways. People were isolated from their families by policies and procedures that served to make families feel unwelcome in services. Service managers failed to report harms that occurred to people, resulting in them not receiving emotional support from family or other supporters when they were in pain or trauma. Families and people with intellectual disability were not consulted about major changes in services, resulting in conflict.

These actions occurred within a broader cultural context, where social policy of the past had encouraged the dislocation of people with intellectual disability from their families and communities, promoting a model where services took sole responsibility for people's care (Johnson and Traustadottir 2005). Despite the more recent policy and rhetoric around consumer engagement, individual planning and the importance of family relationships, the results of this study show that in practice there has been an inadequate shift between the two paradigms.

Lack of adequate concern

A lack of appropriate concern for the harm experienced by people with intellectual disability was frequently expressed. With the exception of key caring individual staff members, participants universally recalled that support workers' and managers' responses to the harm they experienced were less than vigorous. All family participants related instances of injuries or harms that were not reported to them by services – in some cases these were of a very serious nature. People with intellectual disability felt that support workers and managers, in the main, were not interested in hearing about the abuses they had experienced and took little action to address it. People made comments like 'they ignore me' and 'they don't want to listen to me', and one person was called 'manipulative' for reporting the abuse she experienced. These responses compounded the initial abuse experienced by people with intellectual disability and had a substantial impact on their emotional and psychological wellbeing, both in the short and long term.

Living in a state of fear

Living with the threat of violence from co-residents and not feeling vigorously protected by staff was a way of life for all participants who had shared accommodation with groups of people with intellectual disability apart from one. Being intimidated, threatened and terrorised by staff and managers was also a lived reality for seven of the nine people in the study. At times these threats of violence from both other residents and from workers and managers escalated to physical assault. For several people, these experiences were so constant that they amounted to a continual state of fear at some points in their lives.

The level of fear and intimidation felt by people who have been through these experiences does not carry through into the academic literature. The impact of the experience on the lives of people with intellectual disability is diluted when their words are not heard on the page. Those studies that include the voices of people who have been restrained, secluded or otherwise experienced abuse, neglect or trauma have great power due to their immediacy and the authority of the voice of participants (Collier *et al.* 2006; Malacrida 2005).

Withholding basic support and rights

Basic support and rights were withheld from people in a number of different ways, resulting in them going without fundamental requirements for periods of time, and going through a great deal of stress and trauma. This included appropriate foods, emergency medical care, therapies and funding for adequate levels of accommodation and support. People with high support needs particularly suffered from the lack of basic supports, and their family members were frustrated and distraught by the long processes of lobbying and fighting for funding with bureaucratic and obstructive government agencies.

The individual nature of protection/the failure of systemic abuse response mechanisms

Several people talked about key individual staff who had worked with them at points in their lives and who had played a protective role. These staff had all taken a personal interest and built a relationship over time. In the institutional environment, these staff played protective roles for both Jill and Fran, preventing Fran from moving to an inappropriate ward and taking action to address Jill's serious health problems. In the private accommodation arena, Ann recalled the protective role played by a staff member who was instrumental in having another worker who had pushed Ann down the stairs sacked. Only one person with intellectual disability, and no family members, talked about any protective function in services or systems acting to protect them or to respond effectively to their abuse. On the contrary, their experience of complaint mechanisms and policies around abuse was largely negative. This is discussed in more detail in the next chapter.

All participants in this study had support from an advocate in addressing the consequences of their abuse on their lives. This advocacy support was very important for all of them in addressing the situations in which the abuse was occurring. Without independent, skilled support, people may not have left the situations in which they were living and may have continued to be abused – in fact, Jim, Tom and Jenny, who continue to live in more 'traditional' service models, still talked about ongoing problems in dealing with workers, choice and control over life issues.

The academic disability abuse literature appears silent on the subject of 'champions' within institutional cultures who are unsupportive in addressing abuse. Several autobiographies by people with disability, referred to in Chapter 2, raise the importance of allies in addressing abuse. This may be a fruitful area for further investigation.

The volume, range and frequency of emotional and psychological abuse and neglect experienced by participants in this study were such that it has been an unavoidable and inevitable part of their service lives. Eight of the nine people with intellectual disability have experienced it across a range of services and different service types and over many years. It has continued across different policy regimes and institutional or organisational structures and continued despite the presence of systemic safeguards. Discussing the experience of abuse and neglect also raises questions about why this abuse is so endemic and the impact of it on people with intellectual disability. These are addressed in the following sections of the chapter.

Impact of the abuse and neglect

Participants in the study felt the abuse experiences have had a significant and lasting impact on their lives. This manifested in many ways – through people's emotions, their mental health, their capacity to develop and maintain healthy relationships and their cultural connections. It is not possible in this study to distinguish whether or not abuse was the cause of, or consequence of, negative outcomes in people's lives. As their narratives show, participants were complex people, with complicated histories, relationships and needs. Some of these characteristics may have had the effect of making people more vulnerable to abuse or exacerbating the effects of abuse or neglect. Nonetheless, the perceived impact of abuse and neglect related by people is of critical importance – it is their lived reality.

The abuse and neglect that is described occurs across a continuum, ranging from subtle to extreme actions. The most 'extreme' abuses, however, may not be the ones that have had the most impact on the person – they may be one particular instance, a chain of behaviour from a particular abuser or the collage of small insults and hurts over time coming from a range of people, which all participants experienced.

People showed a considerable range of emotions in discussing the impact of the abuse on their lives. Some of the abuses that left lasting pain might be not be considered critical incidents by services, but they certainly seemed to have had an enduring and significant impact on the person at the receiving end. Other abuses that were at a level that should trigger investigations in services, or criminal charges, did not seem to cause as much distress to participants – perhaps because they were better acknowledged and addressed at the time. For some people, it was the fact that their concerns were repeatedly degraded and ignored by managers that caused their distress and that they said were as, or more, abusive to them than the original incident about which they were complaining.

Key stakeholders identified some impacts of emotional and psychological abuse that may not be visible to casual visitors, investigators or auditors. They expressed concern that this abuse, and its considerable impact, would continue unrecognised by outsiders due to the subtle signs of the impact on people with intellectual disability. These included people isolating themselves or removing themselves from painful situations; the 'wearing effect' of continual small abuses that people can't express to other outsiders; increasing anxiety; abrading and degrading of psyche and confidence; damaging of burgeoning relationships (moving staff if residents start to develop a relationship of trust or reliance with them); and trading off dignity for security of service.

There was also a flow-on impact on family members. All family members expressed the view that they were not able to rely on disability services systems to provide care and support for their family member to live free from abuse. They said, in fact, that it proved to them it could not, or would not, provide safe service – evidenced by the number and range of harms that occurred to their family members.

The difficulty for family members lay in the binary position into which they felt forced. In order to remove their family member from a situation that they viewed as inherently unsafe and unsatisfactory, they were required to make some considerable sacrifices to their own quality of life. Ivy, Datu, Patrick and Amanda and her ex-husband all currently spend well over 30 hours every week directly supporting their family member, to make up for shortfalls in funding in their current supported accommodation arrangements. Rose also spends considerable time supporting Jenny and is working hard to try and find another option where she can be better supported.

Horne *et al.* (2001) contend that the prevalence of emotional and psychological abuse and neglect of people with disability is such that the impact of the trauma experienced by individuals also becomes part of a more widespread embedded social trauma. Families are caught up in this wider social trauma. Segregation, isolation and institutionalisation have been traditional approaches to managing disability within the historically dominant bio-medical, individualistic paradigm of disability. It is consistently held in the literature that the propensity of these practices to cause emotional abuse and neglect has been largely unrecognised (Brown 1999; Johnson and Traustadottir 2005). Where families have rejected these approaches as causing damage and harm to their family member, they are left with few, if any, alternative approaches within a disability services system that remains dominated by this conceptual approach.

It is argued by Horne *et al.* (2001) that responses to abuse that involve social repression and denial allow abusive social and cultural practices to continue. In this study, the central place of systems in the emotional and psychological abuse and neglect of people with intellectual disability, discussed in detail in Chapter 8, confirms the multiple layers of traumatic impact caused by this abuse.

The clear and significant negative impact of emotional and psychological abuse related by participants in this study confirms and extends the small literature in the field. Much of the literature focuses on detection, response and prevention of harm, with little focus on impact. The results of this study accord with the few studies that focus on the impact of abuse on people with intellectual disability (Mitchell *et al.* 2006; O'Callaghan and Murphy 2003). These studies found the consequences to be profound and long lasting, and made links to post traumatic stress disorder. The emphasis in the child abuse impact literature on the damage done to the child's sense of self and their understanding of the ways in which they relate to the people and world around them also has parallels in this study (Glaser 2002; Kairys *et al.* 2002). However, there are clear differences in the experiences of adults, and care needs to be taken not to conflate them.

Resistance and resilience

Great resilience was demonstrated on the part of people with intellectual disability and family members. People with intellectual disability showed their resilience in simply living through the range and volume of abuses they described and continuing to find pleasure in their daily lives. Family participants demonstrated their resilience in their consistent and long-fought battles with services and government departments to create a better living environment for their family member. It took several years for Dan, Jill, Fran, Ann and Jenny to each move into a more responsive, individualised home environment. Amanda's perspective of Fran is indicative of that of several participants. She said: 'Fran is a leader. She has survived horrific experiences in a horrific institution, and now she's thriving – because she has a decent life. She might not know she's a leader, but she is a leader.'

A theme of resistance runs through the narratives – people are not passive victims to their experiences of abuse in disability services systems. Participants drew on many different strategies and methods to 'get through' the difficult periods in their lives.

People with intellectual disability tried to keep their experiences in some sort of context by focusing on the good times they had over the years and the positive relationships with some individual staff and co-residents. They also worked to live in the present and look to the future, which was sometimes hard. For example, Jim felt his experiences had taught him what to expect from services, but had toughened him up a bit, so he felt a little better equipped to deal with potential problems. Craig worked in an area where he could make changes to try and make sure other people did not have the same experiences he had. Ann used focused strategies to remind herself that when she had dreams about her past abuse, it was in the past – she counted what she viewed as her good fortunes one by one to drive the bad memories away.

Family members struggled with guilt and pain over the abuse that their family member had undergone. The lack of hard evidence had often made it difficult for them to take action, and they had channelled their concern into practical action, fundraising for services, completing informal physical therapy with their family member or contributing to parent support groups.

The ways in which people have resisted and reconciled the abuse in their lives are important – both to their individual stories and to the research. Lindemann Nelson (2001) argues that because identities are constructed and damaged narratively, they can be repaired through narrative means. This is done through the counterstory. The counterstory in this context allows people to present themselves as fully formed, moral agents, who have shown strength and resilience in the face of adversity. They are worthy of moral respect by others, and themselves.

This can seen vividly in Tom's experience of having his wheelchair damaged by a support worker to prevent him going to the doctor. His no doubt frightening experience of being dominated and controlled was related as an anecdote about how he had complained successfully about poor treatment, finishing with his comment about the skills of the worker, who was training to be a doctor, 'I told him his bedside manner…sucked big time!' For Tom, this was an example about how he stood up for himself and resisted mistreatment. The counterstories of resistance and resilience that appear in the narratives are a key response to the invalidating representations of people's lives.

That people were able to participate in this study may be due in part to the fact that their abuse is in most cases historical. They are living in safer and more individualised situations now and can talk about their experiences with the filters of time passed and distance. This was also the case in the biographies and autobiographies reviewed in Chapter 2. In the case of research on such a potentially disturbing and unsafe topic for people living in services, the potential for causing distress may need to be balanced against the methodological difficulties caused by asking people with intellectual disability to recollect past events (Booth and Booth 1996; Owens 2007).

It is noteworthy that most disability abuse literature reviewed did not include a significant focus on recovery, focusing more on understanding, defining and responding to abuse. In an environment in which so much abuse and assault against people with disability goes unrecognised and unaddressed, this is a priority. However, it may be useful to draw from the women's and children's abuse fields in their focus on recovery and resilience, particularly for this abuse and neglect, which is so pervasive and longstanding. A need for research and practice that focuses on recovery and resilience of people with intellectual disability who have experienced abuse can be clearly seen.

Understanding why this happens

As discussed in Chapter 2, the constructions of people with intellectual disability as 'other', as damaged, as less than human and as needing to be 'kept in their place' are powerful and dominant modes of social and cultural operation, and they have informed the development of the structures, including the disability services systems, within which people live.

The theoretical understandings of the social, cultural and structural roles and places of people with intellectual disability reviewed in this study hold that people are oppressed, isolated and dehumanised on fundamental levels. The results of the study confirm this clearly. Lindemann Nelson's (2001) concept of damaged identities is very relevant to the experiences of participants in this research. She contends that where an entire group are identified as morally defective or lacking (as in the case of people with intellectual disability), mandatory identities are constructed, where social expectations are set up about how group members are expected to behave, what they can know, what can be demanded of them and to whom they are answerable. This is what she calls damaged identities. Individual identities are subsumed into a marginalised social group experience.

The long history of emotional and psychological abuse and neglect that each of the participants in the study have experienced is indicative of their conceptual position as what Clapton terms 'profoundly irrelevant' (2003, p.541). This is reflected in the study in the focus of the service system on the 'resident' or 'client' category in which people are placed. Residents are different to citizens and are treated differently. They are subject to policies and procedures that govern the way in which they live their lives (Lanoix 2005). They also depend on the vagaries of an under-resourced disability services system to provide staff to support them to live in artificially constructed households.

In the lives of participants in the study, this situation sets up a marginalised social group experience and creates a morally compromised identity. When combined with the failure of policies and practices to recognise, effectively respond to, protect and safeguard against emotional and psychological abuse and neglect in their lives, a high risk of emotional and psychological abuse and neglect emerges. Further, holding people in the 'resident' frame may also contribute to a climate in which the response to abuse by service workers and managers is less likely to be vigorous and concerned.

The conception of people with intellectual disability as damaged, 'Needy Others' (Clapton 2003) is pervasive, and influences the way in which policy and practice responds to their experience of abuse and neglect – particularly subtle abuses that have been normalised within service provision. The identities of people with intellectual disability are damaged by the responses of the service system to their shared experience of chronic, pervasive emotional and psychological abuse and neglect – responses that are lacking in adequate concern, overly procedural and system oriented. A mandatory identity is constructed through this dominant response, in which expectations are set up about how residents with intellectual disability in accommodation services are expected to behave, what they can know, what can be demanded of them and to whom they are answerable. Residents are expected to be compliant; they are expected not to know about their right to complain about emotional and psychological abuse and neglect or to understand it – indeed, some staff may not recognise it themselves; they are expected to endure it as a sometimes routine part of receiving service (in its more subtle forms); and they are answerable to any staff member – permanent or casual, benign or malign.

There is a complex interplay of factors that create a climate in which this abuse and neglect occurs with such regularity. The following chapter considers some of these factors from a systemic perspective.

Chapter 7

What Do These Experiences Mean for Practice and Policy?

This chapter focuses on discussion of systemic factors that may predispose, increase risk or protect against the experience of this form of abuse and neglect.

The incident-based nature of the response of disability services systems to the experience of abuse, and its failure to translate policy goals into practice, means that there is little change to the status quo for people with intellectual disability. The high rates at which they experience abuse and neglect are unlikely to change without a distinct increase in the rates and effectiveness of recognition and response to abuse and neglect at all levels in service systems – from prevention through to protection – from further abuse or neglect. The safety of their services is unlikely to change without large-scale, intensive, culturally driven effort. People with intellectual disability also have little capacity to make changes to their own circumstances, due to the enormous power imbalance between themselves and all other strata of the service structure (support workers, managers, organisations and government). This can be seen clearly in the this chapter, which discusses predisposing, risk and protective factors; and recognition and responses of disability services systems to this harm, including policy, quality assurance mechanisms, legal and complaints frameworks.

Predisposing factors

Together, legislation, funding and policy set expectations about the way that services will be provided to people with intellectual disability – for example, the way that funding can be used and who controls its expenditure; the size and structure of housing available to people with intellectual disability; and the number and type of support staff who provide care. These are important contributing features to cultures or environments that may either protect or predispose people with intellectual disability to experience emotional and psychological abuse and neglect. Several factors are at play here, including the focus of and adherence to legislation; the way in which it is interpreted into policy; policy prioritisation; and resource allocation.

Failure to adhere to disability services legislation

The experiences of participants in this study demonstrated a fundamental failure of the disability services sector to adhere to either the spirit or the letter of both national and state disability service legislation. Both laws and their accompanying practice standards include explicit statements that people with disability have the same human rights as others, and that people with disability have the right to live lives free from abuse, neglect and exploitation.

They require that people receive services in a safe environment appropriate to their needs, and that they can pursue grievances about services without fear of retribution or loss of service. Further, this framework of law and policy details the active duty of care of workers and managers to prevent abuse and neglect of people who use their services.

For none of the nine people with intellectual disability were these conditions consistently met. Stakeholders expressed the view that there were no sanctions imposed for services that failed to meet these standards.

Policy interpretations of legislation that fail to attend adequately to the experience of abuse and neglect

Little evidence is found in the literature that legislation and policy is focused on changing the environments and interpersonal dynamics in disability services that may allow abusive cultures to develop and be sustained (Marsland *et al.* 2007; Wardhaugh and Wilding 1993). This is also reflected in the strong focus on managerial approaches and compliance measures by disability service systems that was found in this study.

In more recent years, adherence to legislation in a number of countries has been assessed through quality assurance mechanisms, which measure compliance against standards. This is usually done through audits of policy and procedures and interviews with key stakeholders. There is a body of literature to show, however, that compliance-based audit approaches are unlikely to uncover the more subtle abuses that feature in the daily lives of people with intellectual disability, due to their focus on measuring the existence of policy and procedure, at the expense of individual outcomes and alternative measures of service quality (DiRita *et al.* 2008; Wills and Chenoweth 2007).

It seems unlikely that current mechanisms to measure the actions of services to protect their clients against abuse and neglect will be effective in strengthening protection or building resilience at either an individual or service level. Reliance on a compliance-based quality assurance regime for measuring quality is also likely to result in measurement of the way services respond to the occurrence of abuse that is formulaic and based on individual instances, with little or no recognition of trends of abuse.

Funder/provider/scrutiniser role conflicts

The multiple roles of the government department responsible for disability services are also problematic in terms of managing an appropriate, effective and consistent response to emotional and psychological abuse and neglect at a government level. Several Australian state departments are dually responsible for funding and providing services to people with intellectual disability, and also for monitoring and dealing with complaints against disability services, both their own and those non-government organisations they fund to provide services. While administratively separated, senior managers retain responsibility for the operations of the entire department. It should be acknowledged that criminal allegations are referred to criminal investigation bodies, but few allegations of emotional and psychological abuse and neglect are likely to fall into this category.

There are fundamental conflicts of role in a government department scrutinising the actions of its own staff in the case of allegations of abuse and neglect. There are also difficulties with a funding agency acting as a scrutiniser of the behaviour of agencies it funds, beyond their compliance to contracts of funding. The UK separation of funding, service provision and safeguarding removes some of these conflicts of role. Similarly in New Zealand and Canada, approaches that separate funding and the provision of service have been developed in multiple ways.

Resource allocation

Financial resources have always been a key concern for the disability sector, both historically and currently. The lack of allocation of adequate resources to support the populations of people with intellectual disability in any Australian state (Australian Institute of Health and Welfare 2006) means that governments have to make difficult decisions about the best use of limited resources. In the process, some important protections for people with intellectual disability are not 'funded into' the dominant funding structure for disability services. In fact, there are indications that proposals for some new congregate models of supported accommodation favoured by governments may increase the risk of abuse to people with intellectual disability (Emerson 2004; Fisher *et al.* 2007a; MacArthur 2003). One group of key stakeholders in this study viewed the funding imperatives of government as, in many ways, a harm minimisation approach.

At the time of writing, Australia is developing a national approach to personalised funding and support for people with disability. Some states have implemented individualised funding programmes, with varying degrees of control of funds and decisions passing from services to people with disability and their families or other supporters. Looking to the UK experience of personalisation, a series of opportunities can be seen in putting control of supports in the hands of the people who use them, particularly with regard to preventing emotional and psychological abuse and neglect. When this harm is difficult to report, to name and to make complaints about, to be able to move supports to escape situations that are emotionally disturbing or distressing may be a very important lever. However, while this may resolve issues at a personal level (albeit at a cost), it does not address either abuse of systemic cause or the need to address the behaviour of particular workers or people using services who may be abusive.

Policy prioritisation

Similar to the allocation of funds, the comparative importance placed on policy priorities has implications for the experience of emotional and psychological abuse. Policy makers know this form of abuse occurs. However, it is not prioritised against other policy imperatives, such as vacancy management, dealing with behavioural issues, early intervention and so on. The choices being made at policy levels about which issues to address have the consequence of neglecting to attend adequately to the emotional and psychological abuse and neglect of people with intellectual disability.

At the level of lived experience, this may result in people with intellectual disability being exposed to risky situations on a daily basis. Sharing tenancies with other people with challenging behaviour, an increasing focus by government on group living and resource allocation that is insufficient to allow individualised supported accommodation options for people with high support needs are all indicators of policy prioritisation that provides conditions ripe for emotional and psychological abuse. All participants in this study had experienced abuse and neglect that was caused or exacerbated by these factors.

Underpinning each of these factors is a key assumption about the nature of disability, which heavily (and to many invisibly) influences the way the service system operates. This gives rise to an elemental discord between the stated aims and the practices within the service system. There has been a shift in legislative and monitoring frameworks that frame the operation of government and service policy in the disability services sector over time. People with disability, historically viewed as devoid of rights, are now viewed as rights holders (Hughes 2007). However, rights often remain inaccessible to people with intellectual disability living in disability accommodation services. People can only claim their rights under certain conditions – they need to know they have rights, they may need support to access them and barriers to accessing rights need to be removed.

Risk factors

In addition to factors that predispose people with intellectual disability to experiencing emotional and psychological abuse and neglect, there are a number of factors that increase the risk of this abuse occurring in their lives. These include enforced co-residency; the lack of change at a high policy level; the way in which legislation may not always act protectively; and the lack of protection for residents in the private accommodation sector.

Enforced co-residency

Several participants in the study had experienced multiple abuses that were due to the enforced sharing of group homes and large residential institutions. In these cases, people had not had the opportunity to meet their co-residents prior to moving in together, had no option to move out and had few or no protections against the abuse or assaults, even when they complained. Being required to share a home with people with whom you don't get on sets the stage for negative experiences under any circumstances, and when people had additional intellectual disability and associated impairments (several co-residents that people talked of also had mental illness), the situation worsened considerably.

There is a high degree of consistency in the literature around the features of effective approaches to accommodation and support for people with intellectual disability, as discussed in Chapter 3. They are fundamentally linked to a focus on the individual and to supporting and facilitating the connection of the person in a range of relationships and with a range of communities of their choosing. Several authors also identify enforced co-residency and a 'vacancy management' approach to housing of people with intellectual disability as risk factors for abuse (Chenoweth 1995; Mansell *et al.* 2007).

In addition to being emotionally and psychologically abused by co-residents, the experience of living in an uncomfortable and sometimes dangerous environment is itself emotionally and psychologically abusive and neglectful. The ongoing tension and interpersonal difficulties, and the failure of the services to address these, created a climate of discontent for some people and distress for others.

Understanding not translated into action for change

A well-developed literature exists on systemic risk factors for the abuse and neglect of people with disability. These include the behaviours, actions, attitudes and decisions of managers and staff; the behaviours of people with intellectual disability; the neutralisation of normal moral concerns; and a lack of accountability. Further combining to increase risk are a lack of scrutiny of the organisation; isolation; poor service design, placement planning and commissioning; and quality of physical care and environment (Marsland *et al.* 2007; Wardhaugh and Wilding 1993).

Key stakeholders who participated in the study amply demonstrated that there is a sound understanding of this form of abuse and neglect among a selection of senior policy analysts, lobbyists and advocates, both within and outside government. While none of the participants in the study were directly engaged in making government policy, they were in a position to influence it. However, there is little evidence of this knowledge being translated into practice or policy. This raises critical questions about why these well-placed stakeholders are not having impact in this area and the barriers in translating knowledge into change.

At a government level, ministers and senior bureaucrats were made aware of the abuse that several participants were experiencing, by the lobbying actions of family members. Yet responses from government to families to resolve the abusive situations were glacially slow, and not responsive to the urgency of the need of people to be safe. While the families of Jill, Fran, Jenny and Dan eventually received funding to support their family member in a more individualised way, the path to receiving the funding was rocky and littered with obstacles. Three of the four still do not have sufficient funding to cover the week's support and rely on family support or enforced co-residency to stretch the funding, which none of them finds a satisfactory or sustainable outcome.

Legislation may not always be protective

The restrictive practices guidelines mentioned earlier are an example of regulation that may not act to protect people with intellectual disability from emotional and psychological abuse and neglect. While the intent of the regulation is to set guidelines for the use of restrictive practices, the weakness of the accompanying legislation and its focus on the protection of staff from prosecution in the event of negative outcomes for people being restrained result in legislation that is viewed by many advocates as endorsing the use of restrictive practices such as restraint and seclusion. Key stakeholders expressed concern that, if the origin of the person's challenging behaviour is caused by abuse and this is not understood by workers at the outset, restrictive practices may exacerbate abuse.

Lack of protection for people living in boarding houses and hostels

People with intellectual disability living in the private residential sector – in boarding houses and hostels run for profit – do not have the same level of protection as do people living in funded services. They have no entitlement to services, few tenancy rights and pay a high percentage of their pension to the owner in rent and board. They frequently live in a marginal environment with a mobile population that includes a high proportion of newly released prisoners and people with mental illness – a sometimes volatile and frequently risky mix of residents. When mistreated, there are few avenues for people with intellectual disability to turn to – there is a small number of tenancy advisory services and some access to disability advocacy services.

Protective factors

A number of factors were also identified that may protect people with intellectual disability against emotional and psychological abuse and neglect. These centre on the involved presence of engaged family or other supporters in their lives and having an active and connected presence in the community, with relationships with people outside the disability sector.

The importance of supporters

Having active, engaged family or supporters is strongly represented in the literature as a critical protective factor against emotional and psychological abuse and neglect, as discussed in Chapter 3. The staunch support and advocacy provided by parents and siblings for the people in this study changed the path of their lives. Two people had limited contact with family members for a time – they experienced years of abuse in large institutions and boarding houses and hostels respectively. When their family members re-engaged more closely with them, and connected them with a very effective advocate, large-scale changes began to occur in their lives.

In the experience of participants in this study, the backing of family or other supporters, such as advocates or an engaged support worker, was a key factor in bringing services to account when abuse occurred. The outcomes for people who had 'strategic complainers' supporting them, compared with those who made complaints on their own behalf, were markedly different and more successful.

Supporters were also a crucial component in safeguarding and developing safe environments, particularly for people with high support needs. Family members' long-term lobbying and vision for a better life for their family member directly resulted in significant change for several people. Without their resolute support, it is likely that they would remain residents in group homes or large accommodation groupings, where they would be at considerably higher risk of emotional and psychological abuse and neglect.

There is an important role for practitioners who work with people with intellectual disability to play here in supporting, maintaining, developing and sustaining these relationships.

The value of community and of unpaid relationships

Being engaged in the local community and having relationships with people outside disability services is protective. There is a significant body of literature that establishes the protective nature of being a recognised member of a local community, with relationships with people who are not paid to spend time with you. While many people in this study remained fairly isolated from community relationships, they were, in several cases, less isolated than they had been while they were being abused. Fran (and Amanda's) experience of a circle of support was particularly demonstrative of the protective nature of these relationships.

Both of these protective factors are about minimising the importance of formal disability services in the lives of people with intellectual disability. Meeting daily support needs are, of course, of great importance, but historical, and to some extent current, service approaches that place services as the central focus of people's lives allow for the growth of conditions in which abuse and neglect can flourish, and where there are few independent watching eyes to observe and prevent it (Clement and Bigby 2009; MacArthur 2003). When relationships and connections with other community members have pre-eminent importance, and the role of disability services is to facilitate that greater purpose, a more coherent function and form for support services becomes evident.

Responses of disability services systems

This section of the chapter discusses responses by disability services systems to the experience of emotional and psychological abuse and neglect. It focuses particularly on systemic responses such policy and procedure platforms, quality assurance frameworks and complaint mechanisms – these are the key measures implemented by the service system to address the problem. Discussion of the service system response is divided here according to the order in which it is experienced, and so recognition of the abuse, response to it and complaints about it after the event are addressed in turn.

Recognition of emotional and psychological abuse and neglect

The definitions of emotional and psychological abuse and neglect contained in policy and procedures of government, complaints agencies and service providers (both government and non government) set an expectation for what people with disability should be able to expect service providers to recognise as ill treatment. The clarity of definitions of emotional and psychological abuse and neglect should (with training) also enable service providers to identify interpersonal interactions that are abusive.

In Australia, state-wide policy within which these definitions sit is broad in scope and includes a focus on proactive strategies and frameworks to ensure that abuse and neglect are recognised and addressed at an early stage. These include recognition of the heightened vulnerability to abuse and neglect that social and physical isolation brings; the need for systems to identify and prevent abuse, neglect and exploitation; and the requirement that early intervention approaches for identifying abuse and neglect take particular note of known risk situations, both systemic and individual. Policies also have a focus on professional development and staff training around recognition and response. Broad-scale information dissemination about abuse and neglect generally takes a three-strand approach, addressing legislation and practice standards, information resources and complaints-based training.

This is similar to the approach of a number of other countries. In several states of the USA, New Zealand, Canada and a number of European countries, emphasis in policy for disability services is on principles around prevention, guidance to response to instances of harm and addressing risk. In the UK, a more multiagency approach is evident, due to the emphasis of the *No Secrets* safeguarding approach. Another feature of the UK approach is the volume of easy English material available for people with cognitive disability on personal safety and a range of abuses.

However, despite the existence of policy and information-dissemination strategies, recognition of emotional and psychological abuse and neglect was problematic in the experience of participants in this study.

There were three key reasons for this. Staff were seen by many family and key stakeholder participants in the research to be frequently lacking in the appropriate training and skills to recognise this form of abuse, particularly in its more subtle expression. Second, key stakeholders also consistently viewed staff as often working within environments where a certain amount of abusive practice is normalised. This was particularly the case with 'low-grade' emotional and psychological abuse and neglect. Where staff lacked the professional and personal capacity to recognise it on an individual level, the system did not provide the cues to recognise and counter the abuse or neglect.

The third factor affecting recognition concerns the impact of the quality assurance systems currently in operation in the state in which the research took place. There are many positive elements to the framework, including the monitoring of a level of service practice and the expectation of a raising of quality of service provision. However, there is also a significant cost to this framework in terms of abuse recognition.

At a systems level, the managerial and corporate ethos that drive the quality assurance models used in Australian states may have a negative impact on individual responses to experiences of harm. Key stakeholders expressed concern that the focus of services was directed to the management of systems, rather than the support of individuals, by the requirements of quality assurance. Monitoring and assessment exercises focus predominantly on measuring the existence of policy, and the adherence of procedure to policy, rather than assessing it against the lived experience of people using services. This was also seen to increase risk. This is consistent with the literature, which finds that a compliance-based approach may be unlikely to uncover the more subtle abuses that appear in people's everyday lives, due to its concentration on the measurement of the existence of policy and procedure, at the expense of measuring individual satisfaction with the quality of service provision (Clegg 2008; DiRita *et al.* 2008). In recent times, financial viability concerns for many non-government services and the increasing focus on contract-based performance and competitive tendering of services have added to this pressure (Clapton 2008a).

The 'benchmarking' of a quality of service through quality assurance processes that fails to recognise abuse, particularly subtle ongoing abuse and neglect, runs a very real risk of endorsing and confirming the practices that gave rise to the abuse in the first place. At the least, it is unlikely to adequately address the cause, recognition or response to abuse and neglect under these conditions.

System responses to emotional and psychological abuse and neglect

A managerial, procedurally driven, 'top-down' culture heavily influenced the responses of disability services systems to the emotional and psychological abuse and neglect of participants in this study. This dominated the way in which bureaucracies, service managers and support workers responded to reports of harm and complaints about ill treatment. Implicit within this is a relinquishment of moral responsibility on the part of individual workers and managers.

It was rare that people received prompt and concerned responses from service management regarding their abuse experiences. In fact, family members related a significant number of incidents in which serious abuses were not reported to them by services – these only came to light through file notes obtained by people with disability and family members using Freedom of Information legislation some years later. The positive responses to abuse in the lives of participants – complaints that had been settled, situations of risk that had been resolved and funding that had been allocated – were largely due to the pressures placed by family members and individual advocates on senior government managers over time and to some key individual support staff. No people with intellectual disability or family members expressed confidence in disability services systems to respond effectively to their abuse. Key stakeholders were also highly critical of the service sector's response. Key stakeholders provided a wealth of further examples of emotional and psychological abuse and neglect. As with the participants in this study, systemic factors were also at the root of the abuse in many of these examples.

The failure of services to respond effectively or appropriately to reports of emotional and psychological abuse connects with the lack of adequate recognition of abuse, as discussed previously. In some cases, service managers were working at balancing the needs of a number of co-residents, all of whom had complex support needs, in a climate of under-resourcing and a shortage of staff. To respond to Jim's complaints of physical and emotional threats by a co-resident by saying that he has greater needs and that Jim simply needs to try and be understanding, for example, fails to address both the abuse he had experienced from the co-resident and the underlying systemic factors that had caused the abusive situation to arise. If four men with complex needs had not been living together in a shared situation that was not of their choosing, the abuse would not have occurred in the first place. It is an exemplar of a management system that responds to the 'problem' of disability without due regard for the moral or educative components.

Systemic abuse is clearly present in the double standards used by services in their differing responses to staff and residents who are assaulted or abused. Key stakeholders described staff being frequently transferred to another facility, provided with counselling or stress leave and, in severe cases, receiving financial compensation for the assaults they experienced. Residents most frequently received little or no action in response to assault or abuse from co-residents beyond incident management. This double standard compounds the original injury and is potentially emotional and psychologically abusive, or at the very least neglectful. Key stakeholders argued that a level of systemic emotional and psychological abuse and neglect becomes the norm in many services, to the point where, according to one: 'there's a level of acceptance in the funding'.

As discussed earlier in the chapter, there is a notable failure of disability services systems to adhere to the spirit and the letter of disability legislation in this area. Services have not acted sufficiently well to protect people with intellectual disability from emotional and psychological abuse and neglect or to respond effectively when it occurs. The range, volume and frequency of abuse experienced by participants and the views of key stakeholders in this study are amply demonstrative of this failure. There has been a lack of due diligence on the part of government, policy makers, and service management to ensure that the services that are set up to support people do not, in fact, damage them.

Despite explicit recognition of the social, cultural and environmental causes of abuse and neglect in policy documents, little evidence of action to address these has appeared in this study. Competing policy priorities, resource allocations and managerial approaches to quality assurance may have mitigated any integrated approach for people living in disability accommodation services. The policy and procedure framework appears to respond primarily to individual incidents of abuse and neglect and to treat the symptoms rather than systemic causes of abuse. It is inadequate to deal with the complexity of the experience.

These broad policy statements show some evidence of a shift in ideology, moving towards an acceptance of social perspectives on disability in the acknowledgement of the causative role of cultural, environmental and interpersonal factors. In practice, however, the dominant policy and practice response of the service system to the emotional and psychological abuse and neglect of people with intellectual disability remains firmly within the deficit or individual approach to disability. It focuses on the problem contained within the individual and resolution at the individual level, and it has devoted limited energy and resources to prevention and protection from maltreatment.

The tendency of the service system to respond to abuse and neglect only on an individual level and to treat symptoms rather than causes of abuse is strongly represented in the literature. The failure of organisations to proactively address risk, and broader systemic concerns about power and its misuse, social constructions of disability and the ambivalence of social attitudes to people with intellectual disability are all key in recognising and addressing abuse and neglect, as detailed in Chapter 3. It appears that these links were made by neither staff nor service management in the experience of participants in this study.

Legal issues

There is a demonstrated lack of response by government to the findings of judicial and parliamentary inquiries into abuse in accommodation facilities for people with intellectual disability over the past 15 years. One institution is, at the time of writing, undergoing some redevelopment after closing for a time – despite two judicial inquiries, the earlier one finding a corrupt culture that was 'irredeemable' and strongly recommending closure as soon as possible (Stewart 1995). Criminal charges were laid against workers and the owners of one private facility following one parliamentary inquiry. However, no systemic changes have been pursued to ensure the safety of other vulnerable adults living in similar facilities.

The question of civil liability also arises around the failure of the service system to protect people from emotional and psychological abuse and neglect. The dominant structure of disability services systems may make it difficult, or even impossible, for individual support workers to meet their duty of care requirements to their clients, resulting in them being legally negligent in their duty if their clients experience harm as a result of abuse of systemic cause. This does not appear to have been tested in Australia, due to the substantial barriers for people with intellectual disability taking legal action on emotional and psychological abuse and neglect (Gibney 2009; Mathews 2004).

Legal avenues do not appear to offer an easy way forward for people with intellectual disability to address emotional and psychological harm in this area. Many of the behaviours that make up emotional and psychological abuse are not criminal wrongs, and it may be that we need to draw upon moral, ethical and rights-based frameworks to understand and address it. Two participants had initiated legal action. Although emotional and psychological abuse and neglect were not the subject of the action, they had a contributory role. There are very significant barriers in the legal system, which may preclude access to it in the first place, even before the question of a successful outcome is raised. However, the legal system is largely untested in this area, and a successful legal case against the disability service system could prove a powerful lobbying tool for change.

It is unlikely, in this climate, that mandatory reporting of abuse and neglect would adequately address injustice and ameliorate conditions for people with intellectual disability living with emotional and psychological abuse in disability services. The literature is divided on whether mandatory reporting regimes in other jurisdictions fill the gap left by service providers and other professionals who lack moral, policy and practice grounding in addressing abuse and neglect (French, Price-Kelly and Dardel 2009; Mathews and Kenny 2008). Such regimes can raise awareness, force higher reporting of abuse and neglect and remove moral 'greyness' from decisions about whether or not to report abuse (Macolini 1995). The risks, however, are that their cost can drain limited resources from community-based responses to abuse and neglect, and they can become quickly overwhelmed with the volume of abuse and neglect notifications (Higgins *et al.* 2009).

Importantly, it is identified in the literature that the duty of care obligations on service providers already require them to actively address abuse and neglect in the lives of people they work to support (Elder

Abuse Prevention Unit 2006). The lack of understanding of existing legal and moral requirements by some service providers, and the failure to apply these, may be a more profitable path to pursue. More vigorous and rigorous implementation of existing legislation and safeguards is likely to be of greater benefit to people with intellectual disability in the fight against abuse than the development of a mandatory reporting regime.

Complaints and redress

Complaints did not, by and large, result in an improvement in the life circumstances of people with intellectual disability. People with intellectual disability who complained on their own behalf were more often penalised for speaking out, often subtly. They did not generally have good experiences of complaining and described their complaints being ignored or minimised (with one exception). Family members, while they did not enjoy the experience, persisted with complaints, were able to take them higher and further and demanded different outcomes. They sometimes complained with a view to long-term change, such as funding allocations for individualised support. Family members talked about damaged relationships with services once they complained, being 'unpopular', feeling uncomfortable and the difficulty of complaining to an unresponsive bureaucracy.

Barriers that stop people with intellectual disability making complaints were high. When complaining internally about abuse within disability services, the experiences of several participants show that retribution or punishment from staff for speaking out about unfair or abusive treatment was common. Mechanisms to prevent retaliation or retribution were rudimentary and were seen as unlikely to be effective in protecting people from subtle retribution. As one key stakeholder put it when expressing his concerns about the lack of vigour in these protection mechanisms: 'There's a thousand ways to emotionally abuse someone, and most of them quite subtle.'

External complaint agencies accepted complaints in a manner that required access to phone or writing and the ability to structure a complaint coherently. No ongoing support was available with the complaint process – there was no advocate to walk beside a person through the process and provide moral support, unless they were fortunate enough to obtain advocacy support through a funded disability advocacy service. Complaints mechanisms without advocacy support are unlikely to adequately deal with power imbalances in this kind of subtle, ongoing, insidious abuse (French *et al.* 2009). Access to Official Community Visitors mitigates this to an extent, although resources are low and visiting not frequent.

External complaints regimes were bureaucratic, and quite regimented in some ways. At a state level, complaint intake was structured according to Disability Services Standards. At a national level, it was focused on the experience of abuse or neglect. The focus of both bodies was on individual complaint resolution through conciliation. Issues of serious or criminal misconduct were referred to other bodies for investigation. The state body was also mandated to have some strategic focus on prevention and education and the national body had an education role only. However, there was little evidence in this study of systemic action to recognise and address pervasive cultural elements of emotional and psychological abuse that may emerge through individual complaints in either body, apart from reporting to senior management on emerging trends in complaints.

Complaint responses that have a conciliation approach have mixed outcomes. Some key stakeholders viewed benefits to people with intellectual disability in receiving an apology, and they saw that workers may benefit from seeing that their actions were hurtful and negative, and that they may modify their behaviour in future. However, several concerns are raised in the literature that a conciliation approach may, at times, feed into the power imbalances that are strongly in play in the lives of people living in formal service environments. This may appear as a lack of rigour in investigation and prosecution where the complainant has intellectual disability (particularly when they are not supported by a strong advocate), and in a continuation of the focus on this abuse at a purely individual level, when so much of it is rooted in systemic policies and practices (Mandeville and Hanson 2000; Wardhaugh and Wilding 1993).

Some questions were also raised about how often emotional and psychological abuse is actually recognised in the conciliation process. Complaints agencies at a state level showed a preference for pragmatically cataloguing complaints about issues that could be termed emotional and psychological abuse as other problems to aid quick resolution. Accordingly, examples were given of issues that were abuses but were termed choice issues or privacy issues. Individual resolution is, of course, important, but this has implications for recognising, understanding and addressing this abuse in disability services. It does not consider the influence and role(s) played by systemic and structural factors. This approach also undermines the authority of the person with intellectual disability and calls into question the legitimacy and relevance of their knowledge (Clapton 2008b). This is a key finding of the research and will be discussed further in the following chapter.

Chapter 8

New Insights Into the Problem

This chapter identifies key issues that emerge from the shared experience of the people who have been emotionally harmed. These concern the central place of systems; the recognition of emotional and psychological abuse and neglect by people with intellectual disability; the cumulative impact of the abuse; and the lack of moral authority accorded to people with intellectual disability in recognising, acknowledging and reporting the abuse.

The discussion in the previous chapter focused on the shared abuse and neglect experiences of people with intellectual disability, the influencing factors that have created and maintained the climate in which their abuse and neglect took place and the responses of the service system to emotional and psychological abuse and neglect.

Within and across each of these areas, four key issues emerge that have particular resonance and importance. These problems cut to the heart of the experience of emotional and psychological abuse and neglect. They have been experienced by all participants in the study. They have implications for policy and for practice in disability services and beyond. Most importantly, they offer new insight into the lived experience of people with intellectual disability and provide valuable information about both the ways in which they have experienced chronic, ongoing maltreatment and the ways they understand it.

These four key problems concern the central place of systems; the cumulative impact of emotional and psychological abuse and neglect; recognition of emotional and psychological abuse and neglect by people with intellectual disability; and the lack of authority of people with intellectual disability in abuse acknowledgement and reporting.

The central place of systems

Participants experienced some abuses that were based in predominantly individual interactions. However, substantially more frequent were their experiences of abuses and neglect that had at their root systemic factors, such as policy directives, unthinking following of rules or humiliating institutional practices. People also experienced abuses that were caused by structural factors, or broad social policy and practice. In many instances these systemically and structurally rooted practices resulted in subtle, monotonous abuses that routinely degraded and belittled people in the study. In and of themselves, these were probably not issues over which people would make a formal complaint, but together they blended into a collage of negative and abusive experiences.

The range, extent and volume of these experiences created a climate in which an expectation of ill treatment was set. A failure of services to respond with concern, haste and vigour was described again and again by all participants. Where abuse was responded to by services, it was done on the basis of an individual incident. Nobody had experience of their abuse being considered by service providers as part of a pattern or trend in their lives. It is clear that emotional and psychological abuse and neglect have been present throughout the 'service lives' of all of the participants in the study, and that it has shaped their experiences and impacted on their self-concept and self-worth.

Many researchers in the child, women's and elder abuse literature contend that emotional and psychological abuse is reliant on a sustained attack on the person by an individual abuser. The results of this study demonstrate that the sustained nature of the abuse that does such damage may also be provided by the *environment* or *service* relationship or the *staff/client* relationship, not the relationship between two individuals. There was comparatively little intentional abuse by an individual 'reliant on a sustained attack on the person's psyche' (Iwaniec *et al.* 2006), except in some isolated instances.

Over time, many of the people in the study did not have long-term relationships with support workers – staff came and went regularly in their lives. However, the bulk of the mistreatment people experienced was categorised as being of systemic cause. Disability services systems provided and maintained the conditions under which abuse was more likely to occur, and failed to respond appropriately when it did happen. The individual actions of abusive behaviour from workers and co-residents in many cases need to be situated inside this environment to be understood. The sustained nature of emotional and psychological abuse and neglect that the literature reports was provided by the structural conditions of the service system.

Many of the features of institutional abuse as defined by these prominent authors have been experienced by participants in this study. However, they have also experienced more personal, intimate insults and hurts in addition to those of systemic cause. Institutional abuse is highly relevant to understanding emotional and psychological abuse and neglect, but does not provide the entire answer to its experience or cause.

The cumulative impact of this harm

The cumulative impact of long term emotional and psychological abuse and neglect was striking in the lives of participants. It played a major role in how they currently live their lives, the relationships they are able to maintain, their capacity to trust others and their ongoing emotional health.

The creation of a climate in which ill treatment is expected, as discussed earlier, allowed for the generation of a collage of small and large insults and injuries over time. As each new experience occurred, another piece was glued into the collage.

These experiences have had a significant cumulative impact on people's self-esteem, self-concept and self-worth. Most of the people with intellectual disability who participated in the study themselves were, at the time of writing, socially isolated and had difficulties forming and sustaining equitable relationships with others, and some of them struggled with mental health issues. They found it difficult to trust people and were often suspicious of the motives of others, such as new service providers. People with higher support needs were also isolated, but less so due to their family involvement. Several had mental health concerns and showed indications of ongoing stress and distress, which their families felt was due to their abusive experiences.

This concept of cumulative impact is critical in interpreting the difference between emotional and psychological abuse and neglect. The mainstream view from the child abuse and women's abuse fields is that there is little difference between emotional and psychological abuse, as both relate to cognition. A minority of researchers from the women's abuse (McKinnon 2008) and child abuse (O'Hagan 2006) fields argue that emotional and psychological abuse and neglect are, in fact, distinct. In this conception, psychological abuse is seen as a deeper, longer-term, power-conflicted form of emotional abuse in which a person's sense of self and social competence is threatened.

Accepting the cumulative impact of ongoing emotional abuse of people with intellectual disability in disability services means that individual incidents should not be the only measurement of abuse and neglect. A series of individual incidents of emotional abuse or neglect, together with inappropriate and inadequate system responses over time, may comprise psychological abuse or neglect and cause lasting damage to the person.

This may occur within one facility or across a number of different services and within one set of relationships or across many staff relationships. One experience of abuse or neglect may be enough to comprise psychological abuse, if it is distressing enough to the person. A series of subtle, low-grade, routine behaviours that are not recognised by services, but are seen by people with intellectual disability and families as degrading, insulting and disrespectful, may also comprise psychological abuse.

This sort of abuse also needs to be understood beyond individual incidents, in terms of the 'service histories' and life histories of people with intellectual disability – the neglect and abuse in their pathway through many services, inappropriate services, unresponsive services; and the failures of the service system to identify their abuse and respond to it. Emotional and psychological abuse and neglect are present not only in interpersonal interactions but also in the failings of disability services systems to protect people's safety and to provide them with a stimulating and nurturing home environment. Ann's path, for instance, through many boarding houses, hostels and funded programmes, is one in which little responsibility for her emotional and psychological wellbeing (in the face of known abuses) was taken by either the disability, mental health or criminal justice systems.

Policy frameworks and systems management approaches (such as quality assurance systems) that inadequately recognise personal experience in favour of a focus on the measurement of the existence of policy and procedure may also play a contributory role here. The strong focus on measuring policy and procedure, and the concomitant weak focus on understanding personal experience, directs the attention of disability services to compliance measures. It minimises the time they have available to address issues of interpersonal abuse and emotional neglect, which they may not even fully understand due to their sometimes subtle nature. This allows abuse and neglect to remain unaddressed in the lives of people with intellectual disability, its impact accumulating more rapidly.

Recognition of emotional and psychological abuse and neglect by people with intellectual disability

People with intellectual disability were able to express very strongly that what had happened to them was something that they had not liked and that they felt offended and violated about the things they had experienced. While they did not, with the exception of Craig, have a language for emotional and psychological abuse and neglect, they had a 'moral' awareness that wrong had been done to them on an emotional and psychological level. For example, Jim remembered 'not nice things' and that 'they make it hard...they didn't talk to me nice and treat me nice' when he complained. Ann recalled that an abuser in one place she lived 'hurt them by being nasty to them', and remembered being 'threatened'.

The subtlety of some abuses, particularly those that are systemic in root cause, led people with intellectual disability, and also some family members, to be unsure of whether they had, in fact, experienced abuse. Some of the abuse that occurred within relationships did not appear to be recognised as abuse by either the abuser or the person being abused. However, people were overwhelmingly clear in the perception that these were wrong actions that resulted in harm and hurt to them.

The existing research around recognition located in the review found that women with physical and intellectual disability did not, in many cases, recognise abuses until they discussed it with others who had experienced the same treatment (Collier et al. 2006; Saxton et al. 2001). The outcome of this study is somewhat different – while people did not have the words to name the abuse, they most certainly had a strong awareness that wrong had been done to them.

Lack of moral authority accorded to people with intellectual disability in abuse recognition, acknowledgement and reporting

People with intellectual disability most often did not have an authoritative place in the acknowledgement and reporting of abuse and neglect in this study. Several incidents were related by participants when they were not believed about their experiences of a range of abuses. For example, when Ann told her case worker about being assaulted, he called and notified her abusers that she had complained and then drove her back to the facility and left her there, numerous times. She was told she was 'manipulative' for complaining about the treatment she received – including abuses that caused lasting physical disability and are now the subject of legal action.

There were a significant number of instances where people complained about ill treatment and were punished, either directly or indirectly, for speaking out. Sometimes this retribution was direct, and sometimes very subtle – being assisted into bed at a more appropriate hour after complaining about being put to bed very early, but staff being curt and uncaring while completing the task; or being told that someone else has greater problems, and you need to be more understanding of their needs, when complaining about threats from another resident.

People with intellectual disability who participated in this study were frequently not treated as having legitimacy by the service system – their voice was seen as needing to be interpreted by staff, complaints agencies or sometimes families or advocates. The response of a complaints body to a question about how they resolve complaints that involve questions of subtle abuse that are difficult to prove was indicative of this view: 'So sometimes, the best that we can achieve is to give the person that lodged the complaint a full and thorough explanation of *what really did happen*' (my emphasis).

The knowledge of people with intellectual disability was at times treated as 'irrelevant', or they were treated as 'irrelevant persons' (Clapton 2003). Their moral authority was called into question – both explicitly in the way that the choice lies with services, staff and managers about whether or not to respond to people's reports of maltreatment and tacitly in the way that reporting systems for abuse and other complaints are developed and implemented.

The failure to recognise the moral authority of people with intellectual disability fits within a social constructionist approach to abuse, which holds that abuse continues due to the extreme marginalisation and the positioning of people with disability as 'other' or as less than human. As discussed in Chapter 2, this allows the development and maintenance of cultural and structural practices that are seen as appropriate for people with intellectual disability, but would not be seen as appropriate for people without intellectual disability.

These practices are consistent with Nunkoosing's (2000) contention that some explanations about intellectual disability are privileged over others. The knowledge of professionals and academics is privileged over that of people with intellectual disability themselves. In the context of abuse, the consequence of this is that the lived experience of the subtleties of emotional and psychological abuse by people with intellectual disability has been largely ignored in favour of the privileged professional explanations of abuse, which focus predominantly on identifying and responding to individual occurrences of abuse in which physical harm has been sustained and on controlling the conditions under which abuse may occur.

There is a fundamental disparity between the responses of disability services systems and the abuse experiences of people with intellectual disability in this study. System responses are primarily geared to discrete instances of abuse or assault, which can be addressed and resolved on an individual basis. The experience of participants in the study is that the abuse they experienced is caused primarily by the interaction of poorly trained and supported workers with systemic factors such as managerial culture, resource shortages, policy priorities which downgrade the importance of individual support and institutional practices. The causes of their abuse are complex and require much more complex and well-considered strategies to resolve than have been delivered to date.

Chapter 9

Implications For Making Change

This chapter draws out implications from the research for making change in the lives of people with disability – in practice, policy and research. It addresses barriers and identifies opportunities for change at personal and structural level and argues for a capacity-building approach to this difficult social problem.

Emotional and psychological abuse and neglect are, in many ways, inextricably linked to other forms of abuse – both in the way they are experienced and in the way they are addressed by the service system. This influences the way that they are conceptualised, recognised and responded to in policy and practice. They are often treated as the 'poor relation' to sexual and physical abuse and neglect. Critical questions are in play around how the experience and impact of this chronic and pervasive abuse and neglect can be better recognised, responded to and prevented.

The high volume, range and frequency of emotional and psychological abuse and neglect in the lives of participants in the study were both alarming and distressing. The results of this research with nine people can only be generalised with caution. However, the participants in this study had very similar 'service lives' to many other people with intellectual disability. Between them, people in the study had experience of a wide range of services and service types and interaction with hundreds, perhaps thousands, of staff over the years. It would be surprising to discover that other people in the service system did not share similar experiences. The results are consistent with the literature on other forms of abuse, which, while varying in range and methodology, consistently show a high prevalence of abuse and neglect. The implication from this study is that this form of abuse and neglect may be endemic in the lives of people with intellectual disability. The practice of support workers needs to understand this and be sensitive to it, respecting the fact that people who have lived in disability services for long periods are likely to have experience of emotional and psychological abuse and neglect.

The cumulative impact of this experience has implications for individual people, for policy and for practice. For people with intellectual disability, there are long-term implications for their capacity to form and maintain relationships, their mental and emotional health, their social isolation and their capacity to trust. While people in this study demonstrated determined resilience in the face of distressing abuse experiences and the ways in which they have moved on in their lives have enabled them to put some of the abuse behind them, the impact remains significant and longstanding.

The policy implications of recognising the cumulative impact of this abuse and neglect are considerable. Prevention and safeguarding against the experience of emotional and psychological abuse and neglect become even more important. A more nuanced response to people with intellectual disability is needed, which is able to respond to the needs of people who have lived within the service system for some time (who are highly likely to have been abused and neglected) and to proactively support people entering the system, to prevent them experiencing abuse and neglect.

A range of policy and practice responses are required to meet short-, medium- and long-term agendas for change. Some require resources or political will. Others can take effect immediately. Still others will never take effect unless a series of preceding steps have been implemented.

This chapter considers implications of this study for the future for people with intellectual disability, for policy and practice in disability accommodation services and for research.

Acknowledging barriers to change

Substantial barriers to action appear to be in place. Key stakeholders, for example, were individuals who were well placed to influence change. They were people with a great deal of knowledge, skill and history. Their understanding of emotional and psychological abuse and neglect was sophisticated and nuanced. They indicated that they were not met with hostility by senior bureaucrats on issues of abuse and neglect – on the contrary, senior policy makers and managers were also concerned about the maltreatment of people with intellectual disability. Yet this knowledge, skill and concern have not translated into successful action to stop abuse from occurring.

Making use of definitions and understandings of this harm

Understandings of emotional and psychological abuse and neglect have been further advanced in this study, through testing the emotional and psychological abuse and neglect framework against the lived experience of people with intellectual disability. This approach has brought together two sets of separate material – the experiences of research participants and academic definitions of phenomena. With the addition of the individual/systemic/structural framework (Penhale 1999), this combined material stands to be a useful tool to both policy and practice.

The framework may prove a useful training tool to assist disability support workers, managers, family members and other supporters such as advocates to better understand the actions that may occur in this form of abuse and neglect. It is important, however, that alongside this, they are also provided with an analysis of the role of systems and social structures in this abuse and neglect. An adapted form may be of use to people with intellectual disability in training and education.

A more complex construction of emotional and psychological abuse and neglect can inform the development of policy for disability accommodation services. This may assist policy makers to recognise, and hence to reflect in policy, both the potential range of actions that can occur and the central place of systems and social structures in this form of abuse and neglect.

Better understanding the risk

The risk of emotional and psychological abuse and neglect happening to people with intellectual disability was found in this study to be increased by several systemic factors, such as enforced co-residency, understanding that was not translated into change at policy levels and the slowness of response of senior bureaucrats to notifications of serious abuse and neglect. There was little evidence of action to prevent or safeguard or to manage risk effectively. There are serious implications for governments in addressing issues of safeguarding, risk and prevention of this abuse and neglect. As the knowledge about this form of harm builds, along with the body of work on protective factors, it becomes more incumbent on governments to proactively address issues of protection from and prevention of emotional and psychological abuse and neglect.

There is a need for disability services systems to develop measures to identify and act on the risk of abuse, before having to respond to its occurrence. As discussed in the previous chapter, elements of disability services culture and environments are known to act to increase or decrease the risk of abuse occurring in the lives of people who live in them. This study has confirmed and reinforced previous research on systemic risk.

Service-based change needs to centre on an increased focus on preventing and addressing risk, more effective recognition and response to the experience of emotional and psychological abuse and neglect and broadening approaches to service monitoring and evaluation. This should be standard risk management practice.

Significant resources need to be allocated for the effective development and implementation of integrated approaches that target social, environmental and interpersonal causes of abuse and respect the moral agency of people with intellectual disability. They require skilled drivers and implementers. Until this is the case, it is difficult to see how substantial systemic change will occur.

The place of power and systems

The experiences that people shared in this study show that this abuse and neglect were diffuse and pervasive and were intimately connected to power relations. The lack of power of people with intellectual disability in both their interactions with staff and in their living environment more broadly, meant that they had effectively no recourse to change their situations. A lack of adequate concern for harm they experienced and the poor quality of care in several facilities, combined with the thoughtless following of policy and procedure by staff, resulted in chronic emotional and psychological abuse and neglect. Against this, systemic protection of people's rights was weak, and their experiences of protection centred on those key individual workers who took on a personal protective role.

Existing responses have been largely oriented to individual incidents of harm (usually physical or sexual). Little acknowledgement of the subtle, insidious and systemic nature and impact of emotional and psychological abuse and neglect has been indicated in legislative, policy and practice frameworks in play in the disability services sector.

The central place of systems in the experience of this abuse and neglect indicates that the bulk of the responsibility, and the work, in responding to this form of abuse and neglect lies with the service sector. None of the people in the study had experience of their abuse being considered by service providers as part of a pattern or trend in their lives. It is clear that emotional and psychological abuse and neglect has been present throughout the 'service lives' of all of the participants in the study and that it has shaped their experiences and impacted on their self-concept and sense of self-worth. The 'sustained' element of attack that many researchers see as integral in emotional and psychological abuse and neglect (Iwaniec 2006; Tucci and Goddard 2003) may be provided for people living in disability accommodation services not by a malevolent individual, but by the service environment or service relationship. The range, extent and volume of these experiences created a *climate* in which an expectation of ill treatment was set.

The measurement of individual incidents of harm should not be the only appropriate measure of emotional and psychological abuse and neglect. There is a need for measures that recognise patterns of abuse or neglect over time, and across services and service types, to identify when people are experiencing ongoing harm and neglect. They need to focus on the person, not on the measurement of systems. In this light, governments, senior managers and service line managers all need to take key roles in recognising, responding to and acting to prevent emotional and psychological abuse and neglect. Further, these actions need to be conceived very differently to the responses in the service sector to date.

However, the lack of personal and systemic power that people with intellectual disability had in this study may be perpetuated without due attention to redress the power relations at play in emotional and psychological abuse and neglect. There is a need to focus on building individual resilience in people with intellectual disability who are likely to experience abuse and neglect. The qualities of resistance and resilience shown by participants in this study were key to their moving on with their lives after abuse and neglect and to balancing the substantial impacts of the abuse and neglect on their lives and wellbeing. It is important that a focus on teaching skills of resilience occurs within a broader context, in which structural and systemic factors affecting the abuse and neglect of people with intellectual disability are actively being addressed. It is tragic to teach people to recover better from inevitable abuse.

The need for cultural change

The need for cultural change was recognised by participants at all levels of the study. People with intellectual disability identified the need for support workers and managers who were more responsive to their experiences; families argued for a service system that supported informal family relationships, rather than replacing them, and allowed control by the person and those who were close to them; and key stakeholders saw the need for recognition of the role of the current service structure in providing the conditions in which abuse and neglect are highly prevalent. They also stressed the importance of developing strong ethical or moral frameworks in individual support workers so that they become an effective resource to people in times of abuse or mistreatment. It was recognised that changing the culture of disability services systems was both complex and difficult. Strategies that had been used successfully to influence cultural change included a focus on relationship building and incremental change; having multiple points of intervention; focusing on both individual and systemic levels; and redeveloping funding and service provision approaches to be more person centred.

Respecting the value of lived experience

While disability services systems, complaints systems and quality assurance systems were lacking in their recognition of and response to emotional and psychological abuse and neglect, people with intellectual disability were in no doubt that wrong was being done to them.

The knowledge of people with intellectual disability about their lives was, in many instances, treated as irrelevant and lacking in moral authority by service workers and managers, and they were conceived as lacking in capacity to make judgements about moral wrongs, particularly abuse and neglect. This resulted in them living with abusive situations, particularly when the abuse stemmed from co-residents. In several instances, this seems most likely to have occurred because workers and line managers had little, if any, capacity themselves to make changes to the living situations of the people who were in conflict. However, their responses of negating and denying the validity and relevance of the abuse reports of participants in this study were morally, ethically and legally wrong. Such responses are driven by scarce resourcing, policy priorities that include enforced co-residency and vacancy management and procedurally based staff training.

These responses allow the development of cultural and structural practices that are seen as appropriate for people with intellectual disability but not for others – institutionalisation, isolation and segregation in their modern forms.

The implications of this are far reaching for people with intellectual disability. The creation of alternate cultural and structural practices for people, based on their experience of disability, allows for the experience of an alternate life, in which it is far likelier that a person will experience abuse and neglect, as the factors that protect against abuse and neglect are less likely to be present. Out of this understanding come implications for policy and practice. The factors that may act to protect people from the experience of abuse and neglect – being embedded in community and having relationships – are not features of created service environments. They are features that a high-quality service environment seeks to nurture, but that are too frequently lacking in the lives of people with intellectual disability.

Responses to abuse have been professionally designed and controlled. There is a need for grass roots involvement in defining, recognising and designing responses to abuse and neglect. To date, there are few research, policy or practice guidelines or education resources about emotional and psychological abuse and neglect that build directly from the lived experience of people with intellectual disability. The place of people with intellectual disability in the abuse landscape needs to be rethought. As well as being victims of this, they are survivors of it. They have important stories to tell, and we have important things to learn from their survival experiences.

The way in which disability services systems have included people with intellectual disability in policy processes also needs work. The structure of formal consultation processes are often exclusive of lived experience – reliant on literacy, engagement with government officials and offices and jargon. It is incumbent on policy makers to gather knowledge and make adaptation into the language of policy, rather than expecting people with intellectual disability to make that leap.

More effective recognition and response to abuse and neglect

Complaints, in the main, did not result in an improvement in the lives or circumstances of people with intellectual disability who participated in this study. Reporting structures for dealing with emotional and psychological abuse and neglect were almost entirely ineffective in resolving abuses in the lives of participants in this study. Their reliance on complaints being initiated by very disempowered people in order to identify abuse; the scope for subtle (and not so subtle) retribution by service providers for complaining about abuse and neglect; and the failure of some complaints staff to recognise emotional and psychological maltreatment are all examples of a system that inadequately recognised the limitations placed on people who were frequently institutionalised by the impact of service practices and policies. This calls out for a new approach.

The legacies of historical policy and practice, combined with low policy prioritisation and unevenly implemented policy frameworks, have combined to result in a patchy response to the abuse and neglect of people with intellectual disability. In some instances, this response appears to be driven more by personal feeling on the part of key individuals than well-designed and comprehensively implemented policy and practice.

Abuse prevention and response schemes need to operate in concert with approaches to service monitoring and evaluation that proactively guard against abuse and neglect. In Australia, where this study took place, there is no overarching adult protection response that encompasses the prevention and response to harm of people with intellectual disability. This has been a subject of advocacy and attention for several years. The experience of the UK in safeguarding shows that the development of a robust, proactive and strategic abuse prevention and response approach can be a central feature in combating the myriad problems besetting the current service system.

Advocacy

Individual advocacy support is needed, both in order for people to make complaints about their experiences of abuse and for ongoing independent support. It is essential that people with intellectual disability have someone to walk beside them through the process of addressing emotional and psychological abuse in their lives. The institutional, systemic nature of much of the abuse also calls out for a systemic advocacy response to protect the rights of all people with intellectual disability living in disability accommodation services. The key findings of this research, particularly the central place of systems, the cumulative impact and the lack of authority of people with intellectual disability in reporting the abuse combine to make people highly vulnerable to the actions of the service system and almost completely powerless to change their own circumstances.

The unresponsiveness of the disability services sector to experiences of abuse and neglect was in part responsible for the moves of five people in this study into alternative forms of accommodation. In most cases, the family members of these people were required to make considerable sacrifices of their own quality of life in order to make up for shortfalls in funding so that their family member could live a safer and more fulfilling life. The experience of people in the study showed that the dominant conceptual approach of disability services systems remains, despite the existence of policy rhetoric in the social model vein, firmly ensconced in the bio-medical model. Although personalised support is in development in Australia (and some participants in the study have experience of this), more innovative models of individualised funding, true person centred planning, or family directed service provision that is fully funded has been slow in this country. There is a big difference between partially funded individual supports and fully funded individual supports. Families and people with intellectual disability should not have to make choices between abusive service or inadequate amounts of better quality service. This is, in fact, a form of systemic abuse and compounds the impact of the original abuse on their lives.

As personalised support unfolds in Australia, opportunities for better support may unfold with closer and more individual focus on the person, their preferences and their needs. Some people in this study related that their lives were happier and more fulfilled living with individualised support, but some were very isolated and were not protected from emotional and psychological abuse that continued in their lives, despite using what were considered progressive service models. Critical questions continue about how to safeguard against the abuse of power relations by workers within individual interactions that are out of sight of the community gaze, how to safeguard against isolation and how to support the development of personal safety in people's lives.

Approaches to service evaluation and monitoring

The matrix of legislation, funding and policy in the disability services arena forms a cultural environment that predisposes people with intellectual disability to emotional and psychological abuse and neglect in several ways. At a high level, the existing policy documents of government reviewed in the study contained broad, proactive strategies to recognise and address abuse and neglect at an early stage and included recognition of some of the social and environmental factors influencing its heightened experience by people with disability. However, there was little evidence of a translation of this policy into practical action. Accompanying procedures remained focused on response to individual incidents of harm. State-wide information resources were highly procedural, focusing on indicators of abuse, service quality assurance requirements and individual assault response service contact details. The experiences of participants did not reflect its successful dissemination.

Over time, the focus of service systems in complying with legislation has moved to quality assurance mechanisms. These managerial compliance systems are unlikely to be effective in uncovering more subtle abuses, strengthening protection or building resilience against abuse and neglect at either an individual or service level, due to their focus on measuring the existence of policy and procedure at the expense of individual outcomes and alternative measures of service quality. The 'benchmarking' of a quality of service through quality assurance processes that fail to recognise abuse, particularly subtle ongoing abuse and neglect, runs a very real risk of endorsing and confirming the practices that gave rise to the abuse in the first place. At the least, it is unlikely to adequately address either the cause, recognition or response to abuse and neglect under these conditions.

The approach taken by disability services systems to monitoring of service quality does not, at present, adequately encompass an understanding of the systemic causes of abuse and neglect. Nor does it allow for the in-depth, qualitative analysis and evaluation that would enable services to reflect on their practice and grow from the experience. There is a need to encourage and foster reflective learning in services and service systems, replacing, or at least augmenting, the current heavy focus on compliance to standards. The lived experience of people with intellectual disability needs to form a significant component of any such framework.

The allocation of limited resources is a key concern for government and the sector. However, in the process, some important protections for people with intellectual disability are not 'funded into' the dominant funding structure for disability services. Policy prioritisation at a high government level also impacts significantly on the experience of emotional and psychological abuse and neglect. Choices made at senior policy levels of government about which issues to address have the consequence of neglecting to attend adequately to the emotional and psychological abuse and neglect of people with intellectual disability.

The lack of vigorous and concerned responses at a systemic level to the experience of emotional and psychological abuse and neglect found in this study has significant implications for policy and practice in the disability services sector and, of course, for people with disability themselves. There is a conspicuous lack of sanctions for breaches of legislation; a failure on the part of government to enforce the requirements of disability services legislation and policy; and soft or non-existent penalties for services that do not meet minimum standards under quality assurance measures – these are all indicators of a policy regime that fails to give due weight to the experience of abuse and neglect.

Better understanding protection

The protective factors identified in this study are consistent with those found in existing research – the importance of active, engaged supporters in your life and the value of community and unpaid relationships. The implications for policy and practice here are clear. Relationships protect people. Policy and practice in disability services needs to be geared to the development of supports that engage people in their communities as citizens, in a range of roles and relationships. However, the control that is vested by others in the lives of people with intellectual disability (often expressed through support) needs to be honestly acknowledged and safeguards put in place to maximise protective features while protecting against the reality that a certain level of vulnerability to abuse will always be present in the lives of some people with intellectual disability. Fyson and Kitson put it well in writing: 'The pretence that such support does not also include an element of control leaves a dangerous gap in which abusers may find an all too comfortable niche' (2007, p.434).

This point is about recognising that developing policy responses to abuse and neglect go well beyond the development of policies and procedures titled 'responding to abuse and neglect'. Responding to abuse and neglect in the lives of people with intellectual disability needs to be a consideration in the development, implementation and review of all legislation, policies, procedures and operational frameworks of disability services. Prevention is more about the creation of positive pathways and alternatives for people with intellectual disability to develop fulfilling and sustaining lives than the closing off of opportunities for abusers to abuse.

The lack of protections for people living in the private boarding house and hostel sector resulted in many abuses over time for several participants in this study. As services are owned and operated by private individuals, few protections are in place for residents. It is imperative that strong protections for residents in these marginal environments are put in place. This is a difficult policy question for governments, as it is situated in a climate of unmet need for services, a diminishing private service sector and constrained resources. However, the private boarding house and hostel sector is comprised of a sometimes volatile mix of people with mental illness, intellectual disability or multiple disability, ex-prisoners, and homeless people (Fisher *et al.* 2007b). It is a highly vulnerable population, and people with intellectual disability and multiple disability are among the most vulnerable to emotional and psychological abuse and neglect.

Attitudes to the reporting of the experience of abuse and neglect appeared in this research as an issue that also has implications for both policy and practice. The experience of family members was, in all cases, that they found out about some abuses of their family member after the event. Some people discovered years after the event that gross abuses had occurred through reading file notes they had obtained through Freedom of Information legislation. Others were informed by service providers who had contact with their family member in other parts of their lives. Service providers, and services, do not own the information about their clients. They have a duty, both legally and morally, to inform the family members of people with high support needs of their abuse and injuries, in order that they might advocate for their redress, provide support to them and protect them from further abuse. For people with greater capacity to make their own decisions about informing family or other supporters, a range of power and control issues were in play, which impacted on their ability to tell people what was happening in their lives. At times these were direct threats, but at other times, people simply had no access to their supporters, or had no language to describe their experiences in a way that would make people take action. These are both policy and training issues, and need to be addressed at broad policy setting, state-wide training and at service operations levels.

Education, training and support

This study found little systematic education and training about abuse and neglect was in place. Little training on either regional or state-wide levels, and no compulsory training, was located in the review. No standalone training resources about emotional and psychological abuse and neglect were located.

Training, education and support is needed on all levels – for workers in their practice, their attitudes and values and their professional development; for service managers; and for policy makers and senior bureaucrats. Key stakeholders and the literature are in parallel in insisting that this must go beyond procedural responses to a deeper understanding of the factors that increase risk, strategies to reduce the occurrence of abuse and protective approaches. Education and training need to connect to an understanding of abuse that better grasps the significance and influence of social and cultural factors. Professional training and education is conceptually ad hoc and incongruent, with a mix of paradigms, management approaches and philosophies influencing both shorter professional development courses and university degrees. The influence of positivist conceptual paradigms and functionalist, therapeutic individualistic models is clearly evident. There is a need for a far stronger sociological approach to people with intellectual disability to underpin professional development and university education that is undertaken by developing senior managers.

Education and support of a different kind are needed for people with intellectual disability who use services; for family members and supporters; and for advocates. People with intellectual disability need education about personal safety and about personal empowerment. Approaches to education need to be tailored to the lived experience of participants, and to be alive to the likely possibility of those participants having experienced abuse. Peer education may be a useful approach, particularly in raising the concept of emotional and psychological abuse and neglect with people with intellectual disability, who may not have previously understood that their maltreatment had a name. Family members and advocates need to be able to recognise abuse, particularly in people who have high support needs, and to know how to take action against it and support the person.

Broad systemic change in response to external recommendations

The demonstrated lack of response by governments to the findings of a series of judicial and parliamentary inquiries into abuse in accommodation facilities for people with intellectual disability in Australia and other countries is damning. There is little evidence of systemic change being pursued to ensure the safety of vulnerable adults living in similar facilities.

Over time, inquiries, reports and research have built a consistent demand for a framework that offers alternatives to the current approaches to preventing and responding to abuse and neglect of people with intellectual disability. Yet there is little response from disability policy and service sectors, which continue to operate largely unchanged in terms of how they respond to the abuse of people with disability. The addition of overarching policy statements that make rhetorical statements of commitment to abuse prevention have little meaning when they are not supported with resources, training and education and practical action to give meaning in the lives of people living in those services.

In many ways it is impossible to extricate emotional and psychological abuse and neglect from other forms of abuse and neglect, particularly in considering the implications of research for policy. The issue of mandatory reporting of abuse and neglect of people with intellectual disability is one such area. The literature is divided on the benefits and disadvantages of mandatory reporting in other jurisdictions. The most fundamental question about mandatory reporting concerns whether it would fill the gap left by service providers and other professionals who lack moral, policy and practice grounding in addressing abuse and neglect (Higgins *et al.* 2009). This gap, as seen in the disability services arena, is considerable. There are benefits in the raising of awareness, increase in reporting rates and removal of 'moral greyness' in making decisions about whether or not to report. However, without substantial resourcing for taking reports, responding and removing people from risk where needed, and for thoughtful and attitudinally based training and education for all stakeholders, such a system will only document the status quo.

Sorry – the hardest word?

In the child abuse domain, the abuse and neglect of children in institutional care has been responded to in several Australian states and other comparable international jurisdictions such as Ireland and Canada. Formal acknowledgement of the wrong done to young residents has been made, apologies given by governments and schemes of compensation administered, albeit not always generously or well (Forde 1999; Kaufman 2002; Ryan 2009).

Despite findings of systemic abuse of a similar breadth and depth in institutions for people with disability (Burdekin 1993; Stewart 1995), no similar schemes have been implemented for people with disability. The profound 'othering' of people with intellectual disability at a cultural and structural level may provide the conditions under which such people are not seen as worthy contenders for compensation or apology, or even where institutional practices are not viewed as abusive or neglectful (particularly in the case of more subtle or structural abuse).

This study has demonstrated that wrong has been done, on a profound level. The research clearly shows that people with intellectual disability experience abuse and neglect at significantly higher levels than other people in the community; that their experiences are responded to with comparatively little concern and vigour; and that this abuse and neglect blights their lives. It builds from a body of literature that consistently supports these results in a broader abuse sphere.

At the very least, an honest accounting needs to be taken of the lived experiences of abuse and neglect of people with intellectual disability, particularly those people who have dwelt in institutional environments and navigated the services system for years. An apology is due to those people – for the abuse and neglect they have experienced at the hands of malevolent individuals, for the maltreatment that was the result of poorly executed policy and procedure, and for the failure of disability services systems to protect and safeguard the rights of people living within it to a safe and fulfilling existence.

Such an apology must occur at a judicial level, to ensure gravitas, legal weight and the capacity to make recommendations to government that have financial obligation, such as schemes of compensation.

Further research

The review of the literature clearly shows that the abuse research landscape is complex and fragmented and is compartmentalised into typologies of disability, abuse or marginalisation. A significant proportion of the scholarship in this literature is normative and builds on already excluding or problematic concepts of disability, abuse or otherness and technically questionable practices, contributing further to the exclusion of people with intellectual disability from full citizenship and moral authority. There is an identifiable need for research that considers 'higher order' issues that are at play here, such as questions of the denial of citizenship, rights, humanness and otherness.

An unmistakable need can be seen for further research that explicitly seeks the thoughts and views of people with intellectual disability on their experiences of emotional and psychological abuse and neglect to extend the small but important body of work that has been conducted to date (refer, for example, to Brown 1994; Malacrida 2005; Sequeira and Halstead 2002). This study adds the voices of nine people to the cohort. However, there are many absent voices – people living with mental illness, people with higher support needs, people who have not yet entered the services system – from whom much could be valuably learnt.

Building capacity

Finally, this book treats emotional and psychological abuse and neglect as a problem within disability services systems. The study considers the experiences of people who live within those systems. However, it must be recognised that there is little acknowledgement or understanding of emotional and psychological abuse and neglect at a public or broader community level and no demand for it to stop. There is a need to step outside of the disability services arena with this issue and to create a level of awareness in the broader community of the frequency, range and volume with which abuse and neglect are experienced. From this, action can be taken to raise community expectations that people with intellectual disability should be able to exercise their right to live free from abuse and neglect.

Approaches are needed that build capacity to resist and deal with emotional and psychological abuse and neglect in people with intellectual disability and in those who support them at all levels – family members and advocates, service support workers and managers. Such approaches need to acknowledge the individual, systemic and structural levels at which emotional and psychological abuse and neglect operate, be based upon sound and ethical research and be grounded in the lived experience of people with intellectual disability.

Underpinning all three levels is the need for the creation and sustenance of protective factors – community-based, individualised supported lifestyles with multiple relationships with unpaid people – demonstrated in the literature and confirmed in this study to safeguard people against the experience of emotional and psychological abuse and neglect.

The importance of individualised, well-developed policy and practice guidelines for services, which are informed by the lived experience of people with intellectual disability, should not be underestimated in a capacity-building approach. While it is critical that workers and managers are provided with education and training that equips them to make moral decisions, rather than to follow procedural pathways, a framework needs to be in place that supports those individual responses and provides a context for them.

At an individual level, a capacity-building approach to addressing emotional and psychological abuse and neglect needs to give priority to developing the individual resilience of people with intellectual disability and those who support them so they can better resist the subtle, pervasive and cumulative impacts of this maltreatment. This is a long-term project. Skill needs to be built in workers, managers, family members and advocates to better recognise this abuse and neglect and to support people through it. Education and training needs to be provided that goes beyond the procedural to develop attitudes and values that support change and growth. Advocacy needs to be resourced and sustained, on both crisis and ongoing bases, to ensure that people have someone to walk beside them through the difficult process of addressing emotional and psychological abuse in their lives. Finally, it is essential that support services are in place and are used by people with intellectual disability who have experienced emotional and psychological abuse and neglect.

At a systemic level, capacity needs to be developed in service management, government departments, ministers, policy makers, analysts and lobbyists to more effectively address the legislative, policy and procedural responses to abuse and neglect of people with intellectual disability. Many of the existing responses remain at the technical level and are missing moral and educative components. Disability services systems need to move beyond compliance frameworks to ensure protection and upholding of the rights of people with intellectual disability to safety and freedom from abuse and neglect. To do this, the priority of the policy focus on abuse and neglect prevention needs to be increased. This research confirms a body of work that clearly tells us that much abuse is systemically caused, and service systems need to respond to this evidence by investing seriously in energy and resources to investigate and respond to this. There is a dearth of knowledge about this area and a small research base. Systemic advocacy that is funded and untied, and can act without fear or favour, can support this aim.

At a structural level, the abuse landscape is highly fragmented, into types of abuse, types of victim and types of crime. There is a need for a concentration on 'higher order' issues that are at play here, such as questions of citizenship, rights, humanness and otherness to develop more informed responses to specific problems, such as the experience of emotional and psychological abuse and neglect.

Responses to emotional and psychological abuse in disability services have, to date, been professionally designed and controlled. There is a need for 'grass roots' involvement of people with intellectual disability and their supporters in defining, recognising and designing responses to this abuse and neglect.

Finally, in the broader community, there is little or no recognition of the volume and impact of these harms against people with intellectual disability. This is not a 'disability land' problem – it is a social problem that affects us all.

Chapter 10

Concluding Remarks

Together, the nine narratives of people with intellectual disability and their families form a complex and confronting collage of emotional and psychological abuse and neglect – a collage of insult and injury but also one of strength, fortitude and resilience in the face of hardship. There is more to this than a victim story. People are much more than their abuse experiences – their narratives reflect this. However, their experiences of emotional and psychological abuse and neglect have, without doubt, changed them and, for several, altered their life courses. The impact felt by this insult and injury, although grossly under-recognised by disability services systems, can hardly be understated. These are stories that we need to hear, to learn from.

The narrative collage approach allowed for the development of multiple pictures of the worlds of participants and their experiences of emotional and psychological abuse and neglect. These experiences, framed through the emotional and psychological abuse and neglect framework, have shown that this form of maltreatment is complex and multifaceted. At the core of them are relations of power and control, which influence and implicate the actions and behaviours of abusers at individual, systemic and structural levels.

Connected to power relations are the key insights from the research concerning the central place of systems in this form of abuse and neglect; the cumulative impact of the abuse; the recognition of the abuse by people who experience it; and the lack of moral authority accorded to people with intellectual disability in the reporting of their own abuse. These underpinning power imbalances at multiple levels, in combination with system failures to recognise and redress the root causes of maltreatment, result in policy and administrative structures that have failed to adequately respond to the emotional and psychological abuse of people with intellectual disability in three primary ways.

First, competing policy priorities, resource allocations and managerial approaches to quality assurance have mitigated any integrated approach to abuse prevention and response for people living in disability accommodation services at the broadest level. Second, in the middle tier, an individualistic, procedural approach to abuse response has masked recognition of the medium- and long-term nature and impacts of much emotional and psychological abuse in the lives of people with intellectual disability. The third tier, at the level of daily service provision, is where the lack of recognition and understanding of the phenomenon of emotional and psychological abuse and neglect are played out in routine actions that fail to adequately acknowledge the fundamental worth and respect of people for whom service is provided – not only through intentionally abusive actions, but most commonly through unthinking following of policy and procedure, through workers 'following the rules'.

An indubitable part of the history of people with disability is social death models – the institutionalisation, isolation and segregation that has been a part of the lives of many people with intellectual disability. These practices are sadly far from gone and continue within different arrangements of brick and mortar. A call is made in these closing remarks to dispute any moral integrity granted to models that continue to take authority from people with intellectual disability and those close to them, and vest it in systems. We need to contribute to change that builds from the lived experience of people with intellectual disability around subtle abuse and neglect, in order to have any hope of understanding how to reframe services in such a way that they do not continue to abuse.

The marginalised social group experience and conceptual positioning of people with intellectual disability as 'profoundly irrelevant' results in damaged and morally compromised identities for people with intellectual disability. When combined with the policy and administrative failures outlined previously, this is a highly vulnerable state. It is just this situation that creates mandatory identities, within which expectations are set about the 'resident' category that perpetuate abuse and neglect.

The place of people with intellectual disability needs to be recast. Their rightful place is not as recipients of policy and practice, but as determinants and recipients. Their authority in recognising and reporting abuse and neglect in their lives needs to be accorded the respect it deserves. Their families and advocates, especially for those people with high support needs, also have an important role to play as allies in altering the culture and practice of the service landscape to make it safer and more responsive.

These nine people are a small group, but their stories are similar to many hundreds of others in their state and to many thousands of their contemporaries across the country. It is likely that there are many, many other stories like these. These lives matter.

References

Atkinson, D. (2004) 'Research and empowerment involving people with learning difficulties in oral and life history research.' *Disability and Society 19*, 7, 691–702.

Atkinson, D. (2010) 'Narratives and People with Learning Disabilities.' In G. Grant, P. Ramcharan, M. Flynn and M. Richardson (eds) *Learning Disability: A Life Cycle Approach* (2nd edition). Berkshire: Open University Press.

Atkinson, D. and Walmsley, J. (1999) 'Using autobiographical approaches with people with learning difficulties.' *Disability and Society 14*, 2, 203–216.

Australian Institute of Health and Welfare (AIHW) (2006) *Disability and Disability Services in Australia.* Canberra: Australian Institute of Health and Welfare.

Balcazar, F.E., Keys, C.B., Kaplan, D.K. and Suarez-Balcazar, Y. (1998) 'Participatory action research and people with disabilities: principles and challenges.' *Canadian Journal of Rehabilitation 12*, 105–112.

Barile, M. (2002) 'Individual-systemic violence: disabled women's standpoint.' *Journal of International Women's Studies 4*, 1, 1–14.

Benbow, S. (2008) 'Failures in the system: our inability to learn from inquiries.' *Journal of Adult Protection 10*, 3, 5–13.

Bennett, G., Kingston, P. and Penhale, B. (1997) *The Dimensions of Elder Abuse: Perspectives for Practitioners.* Basingstoke: Macmillan.

Biben, E.N. and Bearden, R. (2011) *Joint Report of Investigations of Allegations of Abuse and Reviews of Conditions at the Office for People With Developmental Disabilities' Valley Ridge Center for Intensive Treatment.* New York: New York State Inspector General and Commission on Quality of Care and Advocacy for People with Disabilities.

Biggs, S., Phillipson, C. and Kingston, P. (1995) *Elder Abuse in Perspective.* Buckingham: Open University Press.

Bonnerjea, L. (2009) *Report on the Consultation: The Review of No Secrets Guidance.* London: Department of Health.

Booth, T. B. and Booth, W. (1996) 'Sounds of silence: narrative research with inarticulate subjects.' *Disability and Society 11*, 1, 55–69.

Bradley, D. (2008) 'Man v the system.' *Sydney Morning Herald.* November 2, p.15.

Bright, L. (1999) 'Elder Abuse in Care and Nursing Settings: Detection and Prevention.' In P. Slater and M. Eastman (eds) *Elder Abuse: Critical Issues in Policy and Practice.* London: Age Concern England.

Brown, H. (1994) '"An ordinary sexual life?" A review of the normalisation principle as it applies to the sexual options of people with learning disabilities.' *Disability and Society 9*, 2, 123–144.

Brown, H. (1999) 'Abuse of People with Learning Disabilities: Layers of Concern and Analysis.' In N. Stanley, J. Manthorpe and B. Penhale (eds) *Institutional Abuse: Perspectives Across the Life Course.* London: Routledge.

Brown, H. (2004) 'A rights-based approach to abuse of women with learning disabilities.' *Tizard Learning Disability Review 9*, 4, 41–44.

Brown, H. (2007) 'Editorial.' *Journal of Adult Protection 9*, 4, 2–5.

Brown, R.I. (1997) *Quality of Life for People with Disabilities: Models, Research and Practice.* Cheltenham: Stanley Thomas.

Burdekin, B. (1993) *Human Rights and Mental Illness. Report of the National Inquiry Into Human Rights of People with Mental Illness.* Canberra: Human Rights and Equal Opportunity Commission.

Carter, W.J. (2000) *The Basil Stafford Centre Inquiry Report.* Brisbane: Criminal Justice Commission.

Champagne, C. (1999) *Wearing Her Down: Understanding and Responding to Emotional Abuse.* Available at http://216.197.126.32/resources/show.cfm?id=30, accessed on 21 March 2013.

Chappell, A.L. (2000) 'Emergence of participatory methodology in learning difficulty research: understanding the context.' *British Journal of Learning Disabilities 28*, 1, 38–43.

Chenoweth, L. (1995) 'The Mask of Benevolence: Cultures of Violence and People with Disabilities.' In J. Bessant, K. Carrington and S. Cook (eds) *Cultures of Crime and Violence: The Australian Experience.* Melbourne: La Trobe University Press.

Chenoweth, L. (1996) 'Violence and women with disabilities: silence and paradox.' *Violence Against Women 2*, 391–411.

Chung Becker, G. (2008a) *State-wide CRIPA Investigation of the Texas State Schools and Centers.* Washington: US Department of Justice.

Chung Becker, G. (2008b) *CRIPA Investigation of the Beatrice State Developmental Center, Beatrice, Nebraska.* Washington: US Department of Justice.

Clapton, J. (2003) 'Tragedy and catastrophe: contentious discourses of ethics and disability.' *Journal of Intellectual Disability Research 47*, 7, 540–547.

Clapton, J. (2008a) '"Care": Moral concept or merely an organisational suffix?' *Journal of Intellectual Disability Research 52*, 7, 573–580.

Clapton, J. (2008b) *A Transformatory Ethic of Inclusion: Rupturing Concepts of Disability and Inclusion.* Rotterdam: Sense Publishers.

Clegg, J. (2004) 'Practice in focus: a hermeneutic approach to research ethics.' *British Journal of Learning Disabilities 32*, 186–190.

Clegg, J. (2008) 'Holding services to account.' *Journal of Intellectual Disability Research 52*, 7, 581–587.

Clement, T. and Bigby, C. (2009) *Group Homes for People with Intellectual Disabilities: Encouraging Inclusion and Participation.* London: Jessica Kingsley Publishers.

Collier, B., McGhie-Richmond, D., Odette, F. and Pyne, J. (2006) 'Reducing the risk of sexual abuse for people who use augmentative communication.' *Augmentative and Alternative Communication 22*, 1, 62–75.

Conway, R.N.F. (1994) 'Abuse and intellectual disability: a potential link or an inescapable reality?' *Australian and New Zealand Journal of Developmental Disabilities 19*, 3, 165–171.

Conway, R.N.F., Bergin, L. and Thornton, K. (1996) *Abuse and Adults with Intellectual Disability Living in Residential Services.* Canberra: Office of Disability.

Crossley, R. and McDonald, A. (1984) *Annie's Coming Out.* Ringwood Victoria: Penguin.

Daisley, J. (2005) *I Hear More Than You See.* Sydney: Landers Publishing.

Daisley, J. (2007) *Rebels With a Cause.* Sydney: Landers Publishing.

De Heer, R. and Rose, H. (1998) *Dance Me to My Song* [Motion Picture]. Australia: Vertigo Productions.

Department of Health Social Care Policy (2010) *A Vision for Adult Social Care: Capable Communities and Active Citizens.* London: Department of Health.

DiRita, P.A., Parmenter, T.R. and Stancliffe, R.J. (2008) 'Utility, economic rationalism and the circumscription of agency.' *Journal of Intellectual Disability Research 52,* 7, 618–625.

Domestic Abuse Intervention Programs (undated) *The Duluth Model: Social Change to End Violence Against Women.* Available at www.theduluthmodel.org/about/index.html, accessed 2 December 2012.

Elder Abuse Prevention Unit (2006) *Position Statement on Mandatory Reporting of Elder Abuse.* Brisbane: Elder Abuse Prevention Unit.

Emerson, E. (2004) 'Cluster housing for adults with intellectual disabilities.' *Journal of Intellectual and Developmental Disability 29,* 3, 187–197.

Fawcett, B. (2008) 'Disability and Violence.' In B. Fawcett and F. Waugh (eds) *Addressing Violence, Abuse and Oppression: Debates and Challenges.* Abingdon: Routledge.

Felce, D. (2000) *Quality of Life for People with Learning Disabilities in Supported Housing in the Community: A Review of Research.* Cardiff: University of Wales.

Finlay, W.M.L., Walton, C. and Antaki, C. (2008) 'Promoting choice and control in residential services for adults with learning disabilities.' *Disability and Society 23,* 4, 349–360.

Fisher, K., Parker, S., Purcal, C., Thaler, O., Abelson, P., Pickering, E., Robinson, S. and Griffiths, M. (2007a) *Effectiveness of Supported Living in Relation to Shared Accommodation.* Sydney: UNSW Social Policy Research Centre.

Fisher, K., Tudball, J., Redmond, G., and Robinson, S. (2007b) *Research into the Service Needs of Residents in Private Residential Services: Final Report.* Sydney: UNSW Social Policy Research Centre.

Fitzerman, B. (1999) *Through their Eyes: Experiences of Abuse as Perceived by Persons with Disabilities.* Doctoral dissertation. Ontario: University of Toronto.

Flynn, M. (2012) *Winterbourne View Hospital: A serious case review.* South Gloucestershire: South Gloucestershire Safeguarding Adults Board. Available at http://hosted.southglos.gov.uk/wv/report.pdf, accessed 2 December 2012.

Forde, L. (1999) *Commission of Inquiry into Abuse of Children in Queensland Institutions.* Brisbane: Queensland Parliament.

French, P., Price-Kelly, S. and Dardel, J. (2009) *Rights Denied: Barriers Encountered by Persons with Cognitive Impairment to the Fulfilment of their Human Right to Freedom from Abuse, Neglect and Exploitation.* Sydney: People With Disability Australia and UNSW Disability Studies and Research Centre.

Fyson, R. and Kitson, D. (2007) 'Independence or protection – does it have to be a choice? Reflections on the abuse of people with learning disabilities in Cornwall.' *Critical Social Policy 27,* 3, 426–436.

Gibney, J. (2009) *Legal Responses to Emotional and Psychological Abuse of People with Intellectual Disability in Queensland* [Interview]. Brisbane: Queensland Advocacy Incorporated.

Glaser, D. (2002) 'Emotional abuse and neglect (psychological maltreatment): a conceptual framework.' *Child Abuse and Neglect 26,* 10, 697–714.

Goggin, G. and Newell, C. (2005) *Disability in Australia: Exposing a Social Apartheid.* Sydney: UNSW Press.

Goodley, D. (2003) *Structures, Social Constructions and Stories: The Debate Thus Far.* Sheffield: University of Sheffield.

Hall, E. (2004) 'Social geographies of learning disability: narratives of exclusion and inclusion.' *Area 36,* 3, 298–306.

Harrison, J. (2000) 'Models of Care and Social Perceptions of Disability.' In M. Clear (ed.) *Promises, Promises: Disability and Terms of Inclusion.* Sydney: Federation Press.

Higgins, D., Bromfield, L., Richardson, N., Holzer, P. and Berlyn, C. (2009) *Mandatory Reporting of Child Abuse.* Melbourne: Australian Institute of Family Studies National Child Protection Clearinghouse.

Horne, S., Merz, T.A. and Merz, D.P. (2001) 'Disability and emotional abuse: mental health consequences and social implications.' *Journal of Emotional Abuse 2,* 4, 39–60.

Howe, K. (2000) *Violence Against Women with Disabilities: A Review of the Literature.* Melbourne: Women With Disabilities Australia.

Hughes, B. (2007) 'Being disabled: towards a critical social ontology for disability studies.' *Disability and Society 22,* 7, 673–684.

Hughes, Z. (2011) *A Story to Tell.* Dublin: National Institute for Intellectual Disability, Trinity College. Available at www.tcd.ie/niid/life-stories, accessed on 6 December 2012.

Iwaniec, D. (2006) *The Emotionally Abused and Neglected Child.* Chichester: John Wiley and Sons.

Iwaniec, D., Larkin, E. and Higgins, S. (2006) 'Research review: risk and resilience in cases of emotional abuse.' *Child and Family Social Work 11,* 7– 82.

Jenkins, R. and Davies, R. (2006) 'Neglect of people with intellectual disabilities: a failure to act?' *Journal of Intellectual Disabilities 10,* 35–45.

Johnson, F. (2012) 'What is an "adult protection" issue? Victims, perpetrators and the professional construction of adult protection issues.' *Critical Social Policy 32,* 2, 203–222.

Johnson, K. and Traustadottir, R. (2005) *Deinstitutionalisation and People with Intellectual Disabilities: In and Out of Institutions.* London: Jessica Kingsley Publishers.

Jones, P. and Stenfert Kroese, B. (2006) 'Service users' views of physical restraint procedures in secure settings for people with learning disabilities.' *British Journal of Learning Disabilities 35,* 50–54.

Kairys, S.W., Johnson, C.F. and Committee on Child Abuse and Neglect (2002) 'The psychological maltreatment of children – technical report.' *Pediatrics 109,* 68–71.

Kaufman, F.C.M. (2002) *Searching for Justice: An Independent Review of Nova Scotia's Response to Reports of Institutional Abuse.* Canada: Province of Nova Scotia.

Kitchin, R. (1998) '"Out of place", "knowing one's place": space, power and the exclusion of disabled people.' *Disability and Society 13,* 3, 343–356.

Kittay, E.F. (2001) 'When caring is just and justice is caring: justice and mental retardation.' *Public Culture 13,* 3, 557–579.

Kostera, M. (2006) 'The narrative collage as research method.' *Storytelling, Self, Society 2,* 2, 5–27.

Kovener, M. (2000) 'Collaborating to serve victims of crime in Denver: victim service 2000.' *Impact 13,* 3, 23.

Lanoix, M. (2005) 'No room for abuse.' *Cultural Studies 19,* 6, 719–736.

Lindemann Nelson, H. (2001) *Damaged Identities, Narrative Repair.* New York: Cornell University Press.

MacArthur, J. (2003) *Support of Daily Living for Adults with an Intellectual Disability: Review of the Literature.* Wellington, NZ: Donald Beasley Institute.

Macfarlane, A. (1994) 'Subtle forms of abuse and their long term effects.' *Disability and Society 9*, 1, 85–88.

Macolini, R. M. (1995) 'Elder abuse policy: considerations in research and legislation.' *Behavioral Sciences and the Law 13*, 349–363.

Malacrida, C. (2005) 'Discipline and dehumanization in a total institution: institutional survivors' descriptions of time-out rooms.' *Disability and Society 20*, 5, 523–537.

Mandeville, H. and Hanson, M. (2000) 'Understanding caregiver abuse as domestic violence: Systemic change in Wisconsin.' *Impact 13*, 3, 14–15 and 27.

Mansell, J., Beadle-Brown, J., Whelton, B., Beckett, C. and Hutchinson, A. (2007) 'Effect of service structure and organisation on staff care practices in small community homes for people with intellectual disabilities.' *Journal of Applied Research in Intellectual Disabilities 21*, 5, 398–413.

Marsland, D., Oakes, P. and White, C. (2007) 'Abuse in care? The identification of early indicators of the abuse of people with learning disabilities in residential settings.' *Journal of Adult Protection 9*, 4, 6–20.

Martin, R. (2006a) 'A real life, a real community: the empowerment and full participation of people with an intellectual disability in their community.' Keynote paper, *Risk and Resilience* Conference, November. Canberra: Australasian Society for the Study of Intellectual Disability.

Martin, R. (2006b) 'A real life – a real community: the empowerment and full participation of people with an intellectual disability in their community.' *Journal of Intellectual and Developmental Disabilities 31*, 2, 125–127.

Mathews, B. (2004) 'Queensland government actions to compensate survivors of institutional abuse: a critical and comparative evaluation.' *QUT Law and Justice Journal 2*, 23–45.

Mathews, B. (2009) *Legal Redress and People with Intellectual Disability* [Interview]. Brisbane: QUT.

Mathews, B. and Kenny, M.C. (2008) 'Mandatory reporting legislation in the United States, Canada and Australia: a cross-jurisdictional review of key features, differences and issues.' *Child Maltreatment 13*, 1, 50–63.

McCarthy, M. and Thompson, D. (1996) 'Sexual abuse by design: an examination of the issues in learning disability services.' *Disability and Society 11*, 2, 205–217.

McClimens, A. (2008) 'This is my truth, tell me yours: exploring the internal tensions within collaborative learning disability research.' *British Journal of Learning Disabilities 36*, 271–276.

McKinnon, L. (2008) 'Hurting without hitting: non-physical contact forms of abuse.' *Australian Domestic Violence Clearinghouse Stakeholder Paper 4*, 1–15.

Mitchell, A., Clegg, J.A. and Furniss, F. (2006) 'Exploring the meaning of trauma with adults with intellectual disabilities.' *Journal of Applied Research in Intellectual Disabilities 19*, 131–142.

Montalbano-Phelps, L.L. (2004) *Taking Narrative Risk: The Empowerment of Abuse Survivors.* Maryland: University Press of America.

Mumford, B. (2012) 'Panorama's Winterbourne View follow-up shows not much has changed.' *The Guardian,* 30 October. Available at www.guardian.co.uk/social-care-network/2012/oct/30/panorama-winterbourne-view-responses-inadequate, accessed 4 January 2013.

Nandlal, J.M. and Wood, L.A. (1997) 'Older people's understandings of verbal abuse.' *Journal of Elder Abuse and Neglect 9*, 1, 17–32.

North Somerset Safeguarding Adults Partnership (2009) *No Secrets: Policy and Procedures for Safeguarding Vulnerable Adults from Abuse.* North Somerset: North Somerset Safeguarding Adults Partnership.

Nosek, M., Clubb Foley, C., Hughes, R.B. and Howland, C. (2001a) 'Vulnerabilities for abuse among women with disabilities.' *Sexuality and Disability 19,* 3, 177–190.

Nosek, M., Howland, C. and Hughes, R. B. (2001b) 'The investigation of abuse and women with disabilities: going beyond assumptions.' *Violence Against Women 7,* 477–499.

Nowak, M. (2008) *Interim Report of the Special Rapporteur on Torture and Other Cruel, Inhuman or Degrading Treatment or Punishment.* Geneva: United Nations.

Nunkoosing, K. (2000) 'Constructing learning disability: Consequences for men and women with learning disabilities.' *Journal of Intellectual Disabilities 4,* 49–62.

O'Brien, J. (1993) *Supported Living: What's the Difference?* Syracuse, Minnesota: Responsive System Associates and Center on Human Policy, Syracuse University for the Research and Training Center on Community Living.

O'Callaghan, A.C. and Murphy, G. (2003) 'The impact of abuse on men and women with severe learning disabilities and their families.' *British Journal of Learning Disabilities 31,* 175–180.

O'Hagan, K. (1995) 'Emotional and psychological abuse: problems of definition.' *Child Abuse and Neglect 19,* 4, 449–461.

O'Hagan, K. (2006) *Identifying Emotional and Psychological Abuse: A Guide for Childcare Professionals.* Berkshire: Open University Press.

Oliver, M. and Barnes, C. (1998) *Disabled People and Social Policy: From Exclusion to Inclusion.* New York: Addison Wesley Longman.

Owens, J. (2007) 'Liberating voices through narrative methods: the case for an interpretive research approach.' *Disability and Society 22,* 3, 299–313.

Packota, V.J. (2000) *Emotional Abuse of Women by Their Intimate Partners: A Literature Review.* Ontario: Education Wife Assault.

Page, S., Lane, P. and Kempin, G. (2002) *Abuse Prevention Strategies in Specialist Disability Services.* Canberra: National Disability Administrators.

Penhale, B. (1999) 'Introduction.' In N. Stanley, J. Manthorpe and B. Penhale (eds.) *Institutional Abuse: Perspectives Across the Life Course.* London: Routledge.

Pentland, D. and Cincotta, K. (1995) *Doug's Story: The Struggle for a Fair Go.* Burwood, Victoria: Deakin University.

Perrin, B. (1999) 'The Original "Scandinavian" Normalisation Principle and its Continuing Relevance for the 1990s.' In R.J. Flynn and R.A. Lemay (eds) *A Quarter-century of Normalisation and Social Role Valorisation: Evolution and Impact.* Ottawa: University of Ottawa Press.

Powers, L., Curry, M.A., Oschwald, M., Saxton, S. and Eckels, K. (2002) 'Barriers and strategies in addressing abuse: a survey of disabled women (PAS abuse survey).' *Journal of Rehabilitation 68,* 1, 4–13.

Roarty, J. (1981) *Captives of Care.* Sydney: Hodder and Staughton.

Robinson, S. and Chenoweth, L. (2011) 'Preventing abuse in accommodation services: from procedural response to protective cultures.' *Journal of Intellectual Disabilities, 15,* 1, 63–74

Robinson, S. and Chenoweth, L. (2012) 'Understanding emotional and psychological harm of people with intellectual disability: an evolving framework.' *Journal of Adult Protection, 14,* 3, 110–121.

Roeher Institute (1995) *Harm's Way: The Many Faces of Violence and Abuse Against Persons with Disabilities.* Ontario: The Roeher Institute.

Ryan, S. (2009) *Final Report of the Commission to Inquire into Child Abuse.* Dublin: Commission to Inquire into Child Abuse.

Saxton, M., (ed) (2009) *Sticks and Stones: Disabled People's Stories of Abuse, Defiance and Resilience.* Oakland, California: World Institute on Disability.

Saxton, M., Curry, M.A., Powers, L., Maley, S., Eckels, K. and Gross, J. (2001) '"Bring my scooter so I can leave you": A study of disabled women handling abuse by personal assistance providers.' *Violence Against Women 7,* 4, 393–417.

Seidman, I. (1998) *Interviewing as Qualitative Research: A Guide for Research in Education and the Social Sciences.* New York: Teachers College Press.

Sequeira, H. and Halstead, S. (2002) 'Restraint and seclusion: Sservice user views.' *Journal of Adult Protection 4,* 1, 15–24.

Shakespeare, T. (1997) 'Rules of engagement: Changing Disability Research.' In C. Barnes and G. Mercer (eds) *Doing Disability Research.* Leeds: The Disability Press.

Sherry, M. (1999) 'What's wrong with the medical model of disability?' *Interaction 12,* 4, 19–21.

Slater, P. (2000) 'Elder abuse and user involvement: strategic components.' *Journal of Adult Protection 2,* 2, 18–28.

Smith, S. and Ward, J. (eds) (2007) *Bungee Jumping, Lawyers, and Love.* Barwon-South, Victoria: Department of Human Services.

Sobsey, D. (1994) *Violence and Abuse in the Lives of People with Disabilities: The End of Silent Acceptance?* Baltimore: Paul H Brookes.

Stancliffe, R.J. and Keane, S. (2000) 'Outcomes and costs of community living: a matched comparison of group homes and semi-independent living.' *Journal of Intellectual and Developmental Disability 25,* 4, 281–305.

Stanger, M. (2004) *Permission to Shine – The Gift.* Brisbane: Meriel Stanger [self published].

Stefansdottir, G. and Traustadottir, R. (2006) 'Resilience and Resistance in the Life Histories of Three Women with Learning Difficulties in Iceland.' In D. Mitchell, R. Traustadottir, R. Chapman, L. Townson, N. Ingham and S. Ledger (eds) *Exploring Experiences of Advocacy by People with Learning Disabilities: Testimonies of Resistance.* London: Jessica Kingsley Publishers.

Stewart, D.G. (1995) *Report of an Inquiry into Allegations of Official Misconduct at the Basil Stafford Centre.* Brisbane: Criminal Justice Commission.

Taylor, S.J. and Bogdan, R. (1989) 'On accepting relationships between people with mental retardation and non-disabled people: towards an understanding of acceptance.' *Disability and Society 4,* 1, 21–36.

Ticoll, M. (1994) *Violence and People with Disabilities: A Review of the Literature.* Ontario: The Roeher Institute.

Ticoll, M. (1995) 'Violence against people with disabilities: getting out of harm's way.' Paper presented to conference *Speaking out Against Abuse in Institutions: Advocating for the Rights of People with Disabilities.* Montreal: Disability-Life-Dignity and McGill University.

Tomison, A.M. and Tucci, J. (1997) 'Emotional abuse: the hidden form of maltreatment.' *Issues in Child Abuse Prevention 8,* 1. Available at www.aifs.gov.au/nch/pubs/issues/issues8/issues8.html, accessed 23 March 2007.

Tregaskis, C. (2002) 'Social model theory: the story so far...' *Disability and Society 17,* 4, 457–470.

Tregaskis, C. and Goodley, D. (2005) 'Disability research by disabled and non-disabled people: towards a relational methodology of research production.' *International Journal of Social Research Methodology 8,* 5, 363–374.

Tucci, J. and Goddard, C. (2003) 'Emotional abuse of children: a study of the narratives in protective assessment and intervention.' Paper presented to conference *Many Voices, Many Choices: Ninth Australasian Conference on Child Abuse and Neglect.* Sydney: Australian Childhood Foundation.

UK Department of Health and UK Home Office (2000) *No Secrets: Guidance on Developing and Implementing Multi-agency Policies and Procedures to Protect Vulnerable Adults from Abuse.* London: UK Department of Health and Home Office.

United Nations (2008) *United Nations Convention on the Rights of Persons with Disabilities.* Geneva: *United Nations.*

Vieth, V. (2004) 'When words hurt: investigating and proving a case of psychological maltreatment.' *Reasonable Efforts 2,* 1. Available at www.ndaa.org/reasonable_efforts_v2no1.html, accessed on 21 March 2013.

Wardhaugh, J. and Wilding, P. (1993) 'Towards an explanation of the corruption of care.' *Critical Social Policy 13,* 37, 4–31.

White, C., Holland, E., Marsland, D. and Oakes, P. (2003) 'The identification of environments and cultures that promote the abuse of people with intellectual disabilities: a review of the literature.' *Journal of Applied Research in Intellectual Disabilities 19,* 1–9.

Wills, R. and Chenoweth, L. (2007) 'Support or Compliance?' In P. O'Brien and M. Sullivan (eds) *Allies in Emancipation: Shifting from Providing Service to Being of Support.* Auckland: Thompson Dunmore Press.

Women With Disabilities Australia (WWDA) (2007) *Forgotten Sisters: A Global Review of Violence Against Women with Disabilities.* Hobart: Women With Disabilities Australia.

Subject Index

Author Index